GoodFood
Easy baking recipes

10 9 8

Published in 2012 by BBC Books, an imprint of Ebury Publishing
A Random House Group company

The Random House Group Limited
Reg. No. 954009

Addresses for companies within the Random House Group can be found at www.randomhouse.co.uk

A CIP catalogue record for this book is available from the British Library

Penguin Random House is committed to a sustainable future for our business, our readers and our planet. This book is made from Forest Stewardship Council® certified paper.

To buy books by your favourite authors and register for offers visit www.randomhouse.co.uk

Printed and bound by Firmengruppe APPL, aprinta druck, Wemding, Germany
Colour origination by Dot Gradations Ltd, UK

Commissioning Editor: Muna Reyal
Project Editor: Joe Cottington
Designer: Kathryn Gammon
Production: Rebecca Jones
Picture Researcher: Gabby Harrington

ISBN: 9781849904704

Picture credits

BBC *Good Food* magazine and BBC Books would like to thank the following people for providing photos. While every effort has been made to trace and acknowledge all photographers, we should like to apologise should there be any errors or omissions.

Carolyn Barber p79; Peter Cassidy p13, p59, p91, p111, p115, p125, p167; Will Heap p17, p19, p53, p77, p87, p101, p119, p143, p151, p155, p175, p191, p207, p211; Gareth Morgans p21, p23, p27, p45, p49, p57, p63, p129, p149, p153, p177; David Munns p31, p69, p75, p97, p123, p173, p179, p189, p197; Myles New p11, p25, p29, p33, p37, p43, p93, p99, p131, p137, p145, p147, p163, p169, p181, p185, p187, p201, p205, p209; Stuart Ovenden p109, p183, p195; Lis Parsons p15, p41, p47, p65, p67, p71, p73, p83, p95, p107, p121, p161, p165, p203; Maja Smend p35, p55, p81, p85, p89, p103, p105, p117, p127, p135, p141, p159, p171; Yuki Sugiura p157; Philip Webb p39, p51, p61, p113, p133, p139, p193, p199

All the recipes in this book were created by the editorial team at *Good Food* and by regular contributors to BBC magazines.

baking

GoodFood
Easy baking recipes

Editor **Sarah Cook**

BOOKS

Contents

Introduction

Baking seems to be the nation's favourite pastime at the moment, and rightly so – what can be nicer than a relaxing afternoon spent in the kitchen making a homemade cake, cookie or loaf of bread, then sharing it with family or friends? It's no wonder that more and more people are taking up the hobby, which is why we've put together this little book full of simple bakes. Ideal for a beginner, but with lots of deliciously different ideas and slightly more challenging recipes for those who've had a little extra practice, or just want to show off!

We've got plenty of yummy treats to fill the biscuit tin, as well as lovely ideas for an afternoon tea – whether you're impressing the girls with something cute and dainty, or just want a slab of something old-fashioned and comforting to munch on with a cuppa. There are classics for Christmas, Easter and Halloween, and plenty of cakes special enough to celebrate a birthday with too. And if that isn't enough we've added some gorgeous savoury bakes, and lots of ideas perfect for making for, or with, the kids.

Before you start grabbing bowls and whisks, turn the page and have a good read of my notes. Not only will you find the usual conversion charts, but lots of essential baking tips that'll help to make the recipes a success every time.

So what are you waiting for? Grab that pinny, pop on the oven and bake away!

Sarah

Sarah Cook

Notes and conversion tables

TIPS ON SUCCESSFUL BAKING

• Egg sizes are stated on recipes where this information is important – if you don't use the stated size the success of the recipe will be affected. These sizes are correct for UK and Australia. In America, however, where the recipe states large use extra large, and where medium use large.

• The best results come from eggs at room temperature.

• Where instructed to grease a tin, use the same fat that's in the bake – usually butter or a flavourless oil.

• Line tins with greaseproof paper or baking parchment. Draw round the tins for the bases, then line the sides with one long strip. Loaf tins are best lined with two criss-crossing strips.

• To test if a cake is done, poke a skewer in the middle. If the skewer comes out clean it's ready, if wet mixture clings to it, it needs to continue baking. Return to the oven for 5–10 minute stages, depending on how close the cake is to being done.

OVEN TEMPERATURES

Gas	°C	°C Fan	°F	Oven temp.
2	150	130	300	Cool or slow
3	160	140	325	Warm
4	180	160	350	Moderate
5	190	170	375	Moderately hot
6	200	180	400	Fairly hot
7	220	200	425	Hot
8	230	210	450	Very hot
9	240	220	475	Very hot

NOTES ON THE RECIPES

• Wash fresh produce before preparation.

• Recipes contain nutritional analyses for 'sugar', which means the total sugar content including all natural sugars in the ingredients, unless otherwise stated.

SPOON MEASURES

Spoon measurements are level unless otherwise specified.

• 1 teaspoon (tsp) = 5ml

• 1 tablespoon (tbsp) = 15ml

• 1 Australian tablespoon = 20ml (cooks in Australia should measure 3 teaspoons where 1 tablespoon is specified in a recipe)

APPROXIMATE WEIGHT CONVERSIONS
• All the recipes in this book list both imperial and metric measurements. Conversions are approximate and have been rounded up or down. Follow one set of measurements only; do not mix the two.
• Cup measurements, which are used by cooks in Australia and America, have not been listed here as they vary from ingredient to ingredient. Kitchen scales should be used to measure dry/solid ingredients.

APPROXIMATE LIQUID CONVERSIONS

metric	imperial	AUS	US
50ml	2fl oz	¼ cup	¼ cup
125ml	4fl oz	½ cup	½ cup
175ml	6fl oz	¾ cup	¾ cup
225ml	8fl oz	1 cup	1 cup
300ml	10fl oz/½ pint	½ pint	1¼ cups
450ml	16fl oz	2 cups	2 cups/1 pint
600ml	20fl oz/1 pint	1 pint	2½ cups
1 litre	35fl oz/1¾ pints	1¾ pints	1 quart

Good Food is concerned about sustainable sourcing and animal welfare. Where possible, humanely reared meats, sustainably caught fish (see fishonline.org for further information from the Marine Conservation Society) and free-range chickens and eggs are used when recipes are originally tested.

Victoria sponge

Everybody's favourite and so, so easy! We've added a layer of cream to make this classic even better.

TAKES 40 MINUTES, PLUS COOLING

● **CUTS INTO 8–10 SLICES**

200g/7oz unsalted butter, softened, plus extra for greasing
200g/7oz caster sugar
4 medium eggs
200g/7oz self-raising flour, plus extra for dusting
about 6 tbsp raspberry jam
250ml/9fl oz double cream
½ tsp vanilla extract
1 tbsp icing sugar, plus extra for dusting

1 Heat oven to 190C/170C fan/gas 5. Grease and flour two 20cm-round sandwich tins. Put the butter and caster sugar into a bowl and beat well to a creamy consistency. Slowly beat in the eggs, one by one, then fold in the flour and mix well.

2 Divide the mix between the cake tins, put into the oven and bake for about 20 minutes until risen and golden brown. The cakes should spring back when gently pushed in the middle. When ready, remove from the oven and allow to cool for 5 minutes in the tin, before turning out on to a wire rack until completely cool.

3 Spread the jam on to the top of one cake. Put the cream, vanilla and icing sugar into a big bowl and beat with an electric whisk until lightly whipped – so it just holds its shape. Spread on top of the jam, sandwich the second cake on top and dust with the extra icing sugar.

PER SLICE (8) 599 kcals, protein 6g, carbs 56g, fat 40g, sat fat 23g, fibre 1g, sugar 38g, salt 0.35g

Eccles cakes

Enjoy while still warm, or cold, with a cup of tea; if you like, eat with a wedge of hard, tangy cheese such as a strong Cheddar or Lancashire.

TAKES ABOUT 1½ HOURS • MAKES 10

500g pack all-butter puff pastry
1 egg white, lightly beaten with a fork until frothy
3 tbsp preserving sugar or roughly crushed sugar cubes

FOR THE FILLING

25g/1oz butter
175g/6oz currants
50g/2oz chopped mixed peel
100g/4oz light muscovado sugar
1 tsp each ground cinnamon, ground ginger and mixed spice
zest 1 lemon and 1 orange, plus 2 tbsp orange juice

1 Heat oven to 220C/200C fan/gas 7. To make the filling, melt the butter in a large pan. Take it off the heat and stir in all the other filling ingredients until well mixed.

2 Roll the pastry out until it's just a little thicker than a £1 coin and cut out 10 rounds about 12cm wide. Re-roll the trimmings if needed.

3 Put a good heaped tablespoon of filling mixture in the middle of each round, brush the edges of the rounds with water, then gather the pastry up around the filling and pinch it together to seal.

4 Flip them all over so the smooth tops are upwards and pat them into smooth rounds. Re-roll each round with a rolling pin to flatten a little until the fruit just starts to poke through.

5 Put on baking sheets. Cut two little slits in the top of each cake, brush generously with frothy egg white and sprinkle with the sugar. Bake for 15–20 minutes until golden brown.

PER CAKE 330 kcals, protein 4g, carbs 47g, fat 14g, sat fat 7g, fibre 1g, sugar 31g, salt 0.50g

Kitchen front ginger cake

Sticky and delicious, this ginger cake actually tastes even better when it's a few days old, so it's definitely worth making such a big one.

TAKES 1½ HOURS ● **CUTS INTO 14–16 SLICES**

300g/10oz butter, plus extra for greasing
400g/14oz golden syrup
1 large egg
140g/5oz plain flour
225g/8oz self-raising flour
1 rounded tsp ground ginger
1 rounded tsp ground cinnamon
120g/4½oz dark soft brown sugar
1½ tsp bicarbonate of soda

1 Heat oven to 150C/130C fan/gas 2. Grease and line a 26cm-round cake tin. Gently melt the butter and syrup with 175ml/6fl oz water in your largest pan. Let it cool for a minute, then using a wooden spoon beat in the egg, followed by the flours, spices, sugar and bicarbonate of soda. Pour the mixture into the prepared tin.

2 Bake for 1 hour, then test the cake by inserting a cocktail stick into the middle – it should come out clean. If not, bake for a further 5 minutes and test again. Turn out on to a wire rack to cool.

PER SLICE (14) 369 kcals, protein 3g, carbs 48g, fat 18g, sat fat 11g, fibre 1g, sugar 30g, salt 0.90g

Cherry scones

Best eaten on the day you make them. You'll not find many guests who'd turn down a freshly baked scone with a traditional dollop of clotted cream and spoonful of jam!

TAKES 30 MINUTES, PLUS A LITTLE COOLING ● MAKES 12–15

450g/1lb self-raising flour, plus extra
    for dusting
1 tsp bicarbonate of soda
100g/4oz cold butter, diced
2 tbsp caster sugar
284ml pot buttermilk
2 tbsp milk
2 tsp vanilla extract
100g/4oz glacé cherries, chopped
clotted cream and cherry or strawberry
    jam, to serve

1 Heat oven to 220C/200C fan/gas 7. Put the flour, ½ teaspoon salt, the bicarbonate of soda and butter into a bowl and rub in with your fingertips until the mixture resembles breadcrumbs. Mix in the sugar.

2 Quickly mix in the buttermilk, a splash of the milk, the vanilla and cherries, and bring together to form a soft dough. Gently press out on to a lightly floured surface, to about 3cm thick. Cut out with 5cm cutters.

3 Transfer to a lightly floured baking sheet, brush with the remaining milk and bake for 12–15 minutes until golden and well risen. Eat warm or cold with clotted cream and jam.

PER SCONE (12) 218 kcals, protein 4g, carbs 36g, fat 8g, sat fat 5g, fibre 1g, sugar 8g, salt 0.72g

Battenburg cake

This recipe makes two cakes, perfect if you've got a crowd over, but the cakes keep well in airtight containers for 3 days, or in the freezer for a month.

TAKES 3 HOURS, PLUS COOLING
- **MAKES 2 CAKES, EACH CUTS INTO 10 SLICES**

200g/7oz apricot jam, warmed and sieved
2 × 500g blocks white marzipan, each rolled to 22cm/9in wide, then rolled lengthways until 0.5cm/¼in thick
a little icing sugar

FOR THE SPONGES
2 × 175g/6oz very soft butter
2 × 175g/6oz golden caster sugar
2 × 140g/5oz self-raising flour
2 × 50g/2oz ground almonds
2 × ½ tsp baking powder
2 × 3 medium eggs
2 × ¼ tsp each vanilla and almond extract
artificial pink or red food colouring

1 Heat oven to 180C/160C fan/gas 4. Line a 20cm-square tin. Beat half of all the sponge ingredients, apart from the food colouring, until smooth. Bake in the tin for 25–30 minutes. Cool on a rack.
2 Repeat the process with the remaining sponge ingredients, this time adding some food colouring. Cool completely.
3 Measure the height of the plain sponge. Trim one edge then use a ruler to help you cut four slices the same width as the sponge height. Repeat with the pink sponge. Trim all the slices to the same length and brush all the sides, not the ends, with the jam.
4 Sandwich two pink and two plain slices in a cube shape, 5cm from the end of one of the marzipan rolls. Trim the length of marzipan flush with the cake.
5 Carefully lift up the marzipan and smooth it over the cake with your hands. Trim the excess marzipan, then crimp the bottom edges using a fork.
6 Repeat with the second Battenberg.

PER SLICE 524 kcals, protein 7g, carbs 71g, fat 25g, sat fat 10g, fibre 2g, sugar 61g, salt 0.50g

Easy iced buns

Perfect for a kids' party, use whatever coloured sprinkles you fancy – the brighter, the better!

TAKES 45 MINUTES, PLUS RISING AND COOLING ● MAKES 20

500g pack white bread mix
100g/4oz caster sugar
1 large egg
flour, for rolling
oil, for greasing
350g/12oz icing sugar
sprinkles, plus food colouring to
    decorate (optional)

1 Pulse together the bread mix and sugar in a food processor. While the motor is running, add the egg and about 250–300ml/9–10fl oz lukewarm water, until a soft dough forms. Knead on a lightly floured surface for about 5–10 minutes. Leave in an oiled bowl, covered with oiled cling film, in a warm place until doubled in size – about 1 hour.

2 Knock back the dough by squashing with your fist, and divide into 20 even-size pieces. Shape each piece into a sausage and place on an oiled baking sheet. Cover with oiled cling film and leave to rise until doubled in size.

3 Heat oven to 200C/180C fan/gas 6. Remove the cling film and cook the buns on the top shelf for 8–10 minutes. Cool on a wire rack. To decorate, mix the icing sugar with a little water until stiff but spreadable, and add food colouring, if using. Dip the buns into the icing and scatter with sprinkles. Leave to dry.

PER BUN 183 kcals, protein 4g, carbs 42g, fat 1g, sat fat none, fibre 1g, sugar 25g, salt 0.46g

Fruity teacake

Put the kettle on! A slice of this is perfect with a cup of tea, and also a real keeper – it will happily sit in the tin for a week and still be lovely.

TAKES 1¼ HOURS, PLUS SOAKING
● **CUTS INTO 10–12 SLICES**

300g/10oz dried mixed berries and cherries
225ml/8fl oz hot tea, made with 1 tea bag
juice and zest 1 orange
50g/2oz butter
100g/4oz light soft brown sugar
1 large egg
225g/8oz self-raising flour
4 tbsp demerara sugar

1 Put the dried fruits in a bowl and pour over the hot tea, orange juice and zest. Cover with cling film, then leave for at least 4 hours or, better still, overnight.
2 Heat oven to 180C/160C fan/gas 4. Grease and line the base of a 900g loaf tin. Beat together the butter and sugar until creamy, then beat in the egg followed by the flour. Carefully stir through the fruit mixture. Spoon the mixture into the tin, then smooth over the surface with the back of a spoon. Sprinkle all over with a thick layer of demerara sugar.
3 Bake for 1 hour or until a skewer inserted into the centre comes out clean. Leave to cool in the tin, then turn out, cut into slices and serve.

PER SLICE (10) 231 kcals, protein 3g, carbs 48g, fat 4g, sat fat 3g, fibre 1g, sugar 3g, salt 0.27g

Chocolate & almond croissants

Ready-made marzipan makes a quick version of frangipane when heated. If you're not keen on marzipan, make these using just the chocolate.

TAKES 10 MINUTES ● MAKES 6

6 croissants
100g/4oz marzipan, broken into small pieces
50g/2oz toasted sliced almonds
50g/2oz milk chocolate, chopped

1 Heat oven to 180C/160C fan/gas 4. Slice into each croissant lengthways, but don't go all the way through – they should open like books.
2 Sprinkle or spread the bottom half of each croissant with marzipan, followed by 1 teaspoon of the almonds and 1 tablespoon of the chocolate.
3 Close up the croissants, put them on a baking sheet and sprinkle the remaining chocolate and almonds on top. Bake for 5 minutes or until the chocolate has melted. Serve warm.

PER CROISSANT 384 kcals, protein 8g, carbs 43g, fat 21g, sat fat 6g, fibre 2g, sugar 20g, salt 0.67g

Lemon drizzle cakes

These little cakes are so light and lovely, soaked with lemon juice and topped with a crisp sugar crust.

TAKES 45 MINUTES ● MAKES 12

250g pack butter, softened
400g/14oz caster sugar
3 eggs, lightly beaten
250g/9oz self-raising flour
zest and juice 3 lemons

1 Heat oven to 160C/140C fan/gas 3. Line a 12-hole muffin tin with paper cases. With an electric whisk, whisk the butter, 250g/9oz of the sugar, the eggs, flour, zest of 2 lemons and juice from 1 until just combined – don't over-whisk.
2 Divide the mixture among the paper cases (they will be quite full), then bake on a middle shelf for 30 minutes, until a skewer poked in the centre comes out completely clean.
3 Cool in the tin for 10 minutes, then transfer the cakes to a wire rack set over a baking sheet and lightly poke each a few times with a skewer. Pour the rest of the lemon juice over the remaining 150g/5oz sugar and zest of 1 lemon, and immediately spoon this over the cakes. Leave to cool.

PER CAKE 378 kcals, protein 4g, carbs 51g, fat 19g, sat fat 11g, fibre 1g, sugar 36g, salt 0.50g

Carrot cake with cinnamon frosting

Carrot cake seems to be everybody's favourite, and this version is one of the best.
If you remember, soak the raisins overnight instead of just microwaving them.

TAKES 1 HOUR 20 MINUTES, PLUS
COOLING • CUTS INTO 8–10 SLICES
zest and juice 1 orange
50g/2oz raisins
150ml/¼ pint sunflower oil, plus extra
    for greasing
140g/5oz light soft brown sugar
85g/3oz each self-raising flour and
    wholemeal self-raising flour
2 tsp each ground mixed spice and
    cinnamon, plus an extra pinch of
    ground cinnamon for icing
1 tsp baking powder
140g/5oz carrots, coarsely grated
50g/2oz walnuts, chopped, plus a few
    halves to decorate
2 large eggs, beaten with a fork
FOR THE ICING
200g tub soft cheese
50g/2oz butter, softened
85g/3oz icing sugar, sifted

1 Mix together the orange zest, juice and raisins, and microwave on High for 1 minute.
2 Heat oven to 180C/160C fan/gas 4 and grease and line a 900g loaf tin. Combine the dry ingredients then stir in the raisin mixture, carrots, walnuts, oil and eggs with a wooden spoon. Tip into the tin and bake on middle shelf for 1 hour or until cooked. Cool in the tin.
3 Once cool, beat together the soft cheese, butter, icing sugar and a pinch of cinnamon until smooth. Spread over the cake and decorate with walnut halves.

PER SLICE (8) 592 kcals, protein 7g, carbs 51g, fat 41g, sat fat 14g, fibre 2g, sugar 36g, salt 0.83g

Hot cross buns

The secret to a good-looking hot cross bun is making your flour paste nice and thick so that the crosses really stand out.

TAKES 1 HOUR PLUS RISING

● **MAKES 12**

450g/1lb strong white flour, plus 4 tbsp for the crosses and extra for dusting

2 × 7g sachets fast-action yeast

50g/2oz caster sugar, plus 2 tbsp extra to glaze

1 tsp each ground cinnamon and mixed spice

100g/4oz currants

150ml/¼ pint warm milk

1 large egg, beaten

50g/2oz unsalted butter, melted, plus extra for greasing

1 Mix together the flour, yeast, sugar, spices, currants and 1 teaspoon salt. Pour in the milk, 50ml/2fl oz warm water, beaten egg and melted butter, and mix to a dough. Knead in the bowl for 5 minutes, cover with oiled cling film and leave in a warm place for 1 hour until doubled in size.

2 On a floured surface, knead the dough for a second, then divide into 12. Shape each portion into a round and put on a greased baking sheet, well spaced. Cut a cross on top of each bun, then cover with a damp tea towel and prove in a warm place for 20 minutes. Heat oven to 200C/180C fan/gas 6.

3 Mix 4 tablespoons flour with water to a thick paste. Spoon into a food bag, snip off the corner and pipe a cross on to the buns. Bake for 12–15 minutes until the buns are golden and sound hollow when tapped on the bottom. While warm, melt 2 tablespoons sugar with 1 tablespoon water, then brush this over the buns.

PER BUN 242 kcals, protein 6g, carbs 44g, fat 6g, sat fat 3g, fibre 1g, sugar 14g, salt 0.46g

Snow-topped holly cakes

Well-wrapped in paper in a tin, the un-cut, undecorated cake will keep for 2–3 months
– just feed weekly by poking in a few holes and dribbling with brandy or orange juice.

TAKES 3 HOURS, PLUS COOLING
● **MAKES 2 LOAF CAKES**

175g/6oz butter, cubed, plus extra for greasing
200g/7oz dark muscovado sugar
750g/1lb 10oz luxury mixed dried fruit with cherries
zest and juice 1 orange
100ml/3½oz brandy or more orange juice
85g/3oz pecan nuts, roughly chopped
3 large eggs, beaten
85g/3oz ground almonds
200g/7oz self-raising flour
1 tsp each ground mixed spice and cinnamon
250g pack marzipan, halved
icing sugar, for dusting
2 tbsp warmed apricot jam
500g pack fondant icing sugar
8 glacé cherries and small washed holly sprigs, to decorate

1 Melt the butter with the sugar, dried fruit, orange zest and juice, and brandy or more juice in a big pan, stirring. Bubble gently for 10 minutes, stirring occasionally. Cool for 30 minutes.
2 Heat oven to 150C/130C fan/gas 2. Butter and line an 18cm-square tin.
3 Stir the nuts, eggs and ground almonds into the fruit, then add the flour and spices. Spoon into the tin and level the top with a spoon. Bake for 45 minutes, then turn oven to 140C/120C fan/gas 1 and cook for 1 hour more. Cool in the tin.
4 Halve the cake and trim the edges. Roll out each marzipan piece on a surface dusted with icing sugar, until they are the size of the cake tops. Brush the cake tops with jam, then put them jam-side down on the marzipan and trim to fit.
5 Make up the fondant icing, then spread it over the cakes so it slightly runs over the edges. Top with cherries and holly sprigs, then leave to set.

PER SLICE 584 kcals, protein 6g, carbs 97g, fat 20g, sat fat 7g, fibre 2g, sugar 87g, salt 0.32g

Doughnut muffins

Best eaten freshly baked and still warm from the oven – don't expect any leftovers!

TAKES 40 MINUTES ● MAKES 12

140g/5oz butter, melted, plus extra
    for greasing
140g/5oz golden caster sugar, plus
    200g/7oz extra for dusting
200g/7oz plain flour
1 tsp bicarbonate of soda
100g/4oz natural yogurt
2 large eggs, beaten
1 tsp vanilla extract
12 tsp seedless raspberry jam

1 Lightly grease a 12-hole muffin tin. Heat oven to 190C/170C fan/gas 5. Mix the sugar, flour and bicarbonate of soda in a bowl.

2 In a jug, whisk together the yogurt, eggs and vanilla. Tip the jug contents and the melted butter into the dry ingredients and quickly fold with a metal spoon to combine.

3 Divide two-thirds of the mixture among the muffin holes. Carefully add a teaspoon of jam to the centre of each, then cover with the remaining muffin mixture. Bake for 16–18 minutes until risen, golden and springy to the touch.

4 Leave the muffins to cool for 5 minutes before turning them out and rolling them in the extra caster sugar.

PER MUFFIN 229 kcals, protein 3g, carbs 29g, fat 11g, sat fat 6g, fibre 1g, sugar 18g, salt 0.40g

Cherry & almond cake

If you use whole cherries they will end up at the bottom of your cake, so if you want them scattered through the sponge, quarter or chop them.

TAKES 1 HOUR 35 MINUTES • CUTS INTO 8–10 SLICES

200g/7oz butter, softened
200g/7oz golden caster sugar
4 large eggs
½ tsp almond extract
175g/6oz self-raising flour
85g/3oz ground almonds
½ tsp baking powder
300g/10oz glacé cherries
100ml/3½fl oz milk
2 tbsp flaked almonds

1 Heat oven to 160C/140C fan/gas 3. Line the base and sides of a 20cm-round deep cake tin.
2 Beat together the butter and sugar until light and fluffy, then beat in the eggs, one by one. Fold in the almond extract, flour, ground almonds and baking powder, followed by the cherries and milk.
3 Scrape into the prepared tin, scatter over the flaked almonds, then bake for 1 hour–1¼ hours. Cool the cake in its tin before serving.

PER SLICE (8) 585 kcals, protein 9g, carbs 70g, fat 32g, sat fat 15g, fibre 2g, sugar 53g, salt 0.83g

Welsh cakes

You can make the mix up to a day ahead and leave it in the fridge ready to be shaped; once cooked the cakes will stay fresh in an airtight tin for 1 week.

TAKES 20 MINUTES • MAKES 16

225g/8oz plain flour, plus extra for dusting
85g/3oz caster sugar, plus extra for sprinkling
½ tsp ground mixed spice
½ tsp baking powder
50g/2oz butter, cut into small pieces
50g/2oz lard, cut into small pieces, plus extra for frying
50g/2oz currants
1 large egg, beaten
splash milk

1 Tip the flour, sugar, mixed spice, baking powder and a pinch of salt into a bowl. Then, with your fingers, rub in the butter and lard until crumbly. Mix in the currants. Work the egg into the mixture until you have a soft dough, adding a splash of milk if it seems a little dry – it should be the same consistency as shortcrust pastry.

2 Roll out the dough on a lightly floured work surface to the thickness of your little finger. Cut out rounds using a 6cm cutter, re-rolling any trimmings.

3 Grease a flat griddle pan or heavy frying pan with lard, and put over a medium heat. Cook the Welsh cakes in batches, for about 3 minutes each side, until golden brown, crisp and cooked right through.

4 Delicious served warm with butter and jam, or simply sprinkled with the caster sugar.

PER CAKE 138 kcals, protein 2g, carbs 20g, fat 6g, sat fat 2g, fibre 1g, sugar 9g, salt 0.13g

Stollen spirals

Lovely for breakfast either brushed with butter and dredged with icing sugar, or iced and scattered with nuts – or decorate them half and half.

TAKES 1 HOUR 20 MINUTES, PLUS RISING AND COOLING • MAKES 11–12

zest and juice 1 orange
85g/3oz each dried cranberries and mixed dried fruit
550g/1lb 4oz strong white bread flour, plus extra for kneading
2 × 7g sachets easy-bake dried yeast
85g/3oz golden caster sugar
good grating of nutmeg
85g/3oz butter, plus extra for the tin
1 large egg
250ml/9fl oz warm milk
oil, for greasing
25g/1oz pistachio nuts, chopped
300g/10oz golden marzipan

TO DECORATE

melted butter and icing sugar, or icing sugar mixed with a little water, plus chopped pistachio nuts, if you like

1 Stir together the orange zest and juice and dried fruit, and leave to soak.

2 Meanwhile, mix the flour, yeast, sugar, nutmeg and ½ teaspoon salt. Mix in butter, egg and milk, and stir with a round-bladed knife.

3 Knead the dough briefly, adding flour only if you need to. Oil the bowl, return the dough and cover with oiled cling film. Leave in a warm place to double in size.

4 Line a large roasting tin with baking parchment. Roll out the dough to about 70 × 18cm. Add the pistachios to the soaked fruit, then scatter everything over the dough. Roll the marzipan into a sausage the same length as the longest dough side, then place down the centre and roll the dough up. Trim the ends, cut into 11–12 slices and arrange, cut-side up, in the tin. Cover with oiled cling film and leave for 45 minutes until well risen.

5 Heat oven to 190C/170C fan/gas 5. Bake for 15–20 minutes until golden, then decorate as you like.

PER BUN (11) 467 kcals, protein 9g, carbs 80g, fat 13g, sat fat 5g, fibre 3g, sugar 41g, salt 0.40g

Easy mince pies with crunchy-crumble tops

Fifteen delicious festive treats. If you only have one tin, make and bake one batch while the remaining pastry is wrapped up in cling film in the fridge, then bake the rest.

TAKES 50 MINUTES ● MAKES 15

300g/10oz mixed dried fruit
200g/7oz apricot jam
25ml/1fl oz brandy
375g pack shortcrust pastry
little icing sugar, for dusting

FOR THE CRUNCHY CRUMBLE

100g/4oz plain flour, plus extra for
    rolling pastry
25g/1oz icing sugar
50g/2oz butter, diced into cubes
50g/2oz whole almonds with skins,
    roughly chopped

1 Put the dried fruit and jam in a small pan, melt everything together, then stir in the brandy and cool.

2 Heat oven to 200C/180C fan/gas 6. Roll out the pastry to just over £1 coin thickness on a lightly flour-dusted surface. Stamp out circles with an 8cm cutter and press them into the holes of a baking tin – you should get 15 from re-rolling the trimmings.

3 Divide the fruit among the pastry cases then bake for 5 minutes while you rub together all the crumble ingredients with your fingers. Top each pie with some crumble, then return to the oven for another 15 minutes until the pastry and crumble are golden. Eat warm, or cool, dusted with a little icing sugar.

PER PIE 266 kcals, protein 3g, carbs 38g, fat 11g, sat fat 6g, fibre 1g, sugar 24g, salt 0.20g

Fruited soda bread

A sweetly spiced twist on this Irish classic, best eaten just warm and fresh from the oven, spread with lashings of salty butter.

TAKES 45 MINUTES • CUTS INTO 20 SLICES

100g/4oz rolled porridge oats
25g/1oz butter, diced
200g/7oz plain flour
200g/7oz plain wholemeal flour, plus extra for dusting
100g/4oz caster sugar
1 tsp bicarbonate of soda
1½ tsp mixed spice
50g/2oz raisins
50g/2oz sultanas
50g/2oz stoned dates, finely chopped
3 tbsp mixed peel
450ml/16fl oz buttermilk
3–4 tbsp demerara sugar

1 Heat oven to 200C/180C fan/gas 6. Whizz the porridge oats and butter together in a food processor, or rub the butter into the oats in a big bowl. Stir in the flours, caster sugar, bicarbonate of soda, mixed spice, 1 teaspoon salt, raisins, sultanas, chopped dates and peel.
2 Pour over the buttermilk and quickly stir in with a round bladed knife until well combined. Tip out the dough onto a flour-dusted surface and gently bring together into a ball with your hands.
3 Transfer to a flour-dusted baking tray and scatter over the demerara sugar, pressing it into the top of the dough. Use a sharp, flour-dusted knife to cut a big cross in the top, then bake for 30–35 minutes until crusty on the outside. Eat warm or cold, thickly sliced.

PER SLICE 161 kcals, protein 4g, carbs 32g, fat 2g, sat fat 1g, fibre 2g, sugar 17g, salt 0.20g

Syrup crunchies

Full of Great British storecupboard staples, the kids will love these crispy, crunchy biccies. Perfect for filling the biscuit tin!

TAKES 35 MINUTES ● MAKES 20

250g pack butter
½ × 397g can condensed milk
175g/6oz golden syrup
175g/6oz cornflakes, plus a few extra
175g/6oz porridge oats
250g/9oz plain flour
100g/4oz custard powder
2 tsp bicarbonate of soda

1 Heat oven to 180C/160C fan/gas 4 and line a few baking sheets with baking parchment. Heat the butter, condensed milk and syrup in a large pan until melted.
2 Very roughly crush the cornflakes in a bowl with your hands, then stir in the oats, flour, custard powder and bicarbonate of soda, and mix really well.
3 Stir the dry ingredients into the melted butter, milk and syrup until well combined. Roughly scoop heaped tablespoonfuls of the mixture on to the baking sheets. Crumble over a few more cornflakes, then squash them with your hands to flatten them a bit. Bake for 12–15 minutes until golden. Cool on a wire rack.

PER BISCUIT 263 kcals, protein 4g, carbs 36g, fat 12g, sat fat 7g, fibre 1g, sugar 9g, salt 0.76g

Double chocolate shortbreads

These crumbly shortbreads are made from just five ingredients. Don't leave out the chilling stage, though – this is a soft dough and needs time to firm up.

TAKES 25 MINUTES ● MAKES 10
175g/6oz butter, softened
85g/3oz golden caster sugar
200g/7oz plain flour
2 tbsp cocoa powder
100g/4oz chocolate chips, milk or dark

1 Mix the butter and sugar together with a wooden spoon. Stir in the flour and cocoa, followed by the chocolate chips – you'll probably need to mix it together with your hands at this stage.
2 Halve the dough and roll each piece into a log about 5cm thick. Wrap in cling film and chill for 1 hour, or up to several days. (You can also freeze the dough at this stage for up to a month.)
3 Heat oven to 180C/160C fan/gas 4. Slice the logs into 1cm-thick rounds, transfer to a baking sheet lined with baking parchment and bake for 10-12 minutes. Cool on the baking sheet.

PER SHORTBREAD 290 kcals, protein 3g, carbs 31g, fat 18g, sat fat 11g, fibre 1g, sugar 15g, salt 0.22g

Lemon kisses

It's worth buying a good-quality lemon curd to fill these gorgeous biscuits, as something really thick, sharp and lemony will make all the difference.

TAKES 45 MINUTES, PLUS COOLING
● **MAKES ABOUT 20**

200g/7oz soft butter
140g/5oz caster sugar
1 egg yolk
1 tsp vanilla extract
zest 2 lemons, juice 1
300g/10oz plain flour, plus a little extra
    for dusting
½ jar good-quality lemon curd
140g/5oz icing sugar, sifted

1 Stir together the butter, sugar, egg yolk, vanilla and zest from 1 lemon using a wooden spoon. Stir in the flour – you might need to get your hands in at the end.

2 Tip out on to a floured surface and bring together into a smooth dough, then roll out, half at a time, and stamp out 5–6cm rounds. Keep re-rolling the trimmings – you should get about 40 biscuits. Arrange on baking sheets lined with baking parchment, cover with cling film and chill for 30 minutes.

3 Heat oven to 200C/180C fan/gas 6. Bake the biscuits for 8–12 minutes until pale golden, then cool. Once cool, spread half the biscuits with a little lemon curd and top each with a second biscuit.

4 Arrange the biscuits on wire racks set over baking sheets. Mix enough of the lemon juice into the icing sugar to give a runny consistency, then drizzle over the biscuits. Scatter over a bit more lemon zest and leave to set.

PER BISCUIT 202 kcals, protein 1g, carbs 31g, fat 8g, sat fat 5g, fibre 1g, sugar 18g, salt 0.14g

Maple, pecan & raisin oaty cookies

These cookies really have to be made to be believed. You can keep them in an airtight container for up to 1 week, or freeze for up to 3 months – if they last that long!

TAKES 35 MINUTES • MAKES 18

140g/5oz rolled oats
50g/2oz desiccated coconut
225g/8oz plain flour
140g/5oz salted pecan nuts, roughly chopped
100g/4oz raisins
140g/5oz unsalted butter
225g/8oz light soft brown sugar
3 tbsp maple syrup
3 tbsp golden syrup
1 tsp bicarbonate of soda

1 Heat oven to 160C/140C fan/gas 3. Line three large baking sheets with baking parchment. In a medium bowl mix the oats, coconut, flour, pecans and raisins.

2 In a small pan, melt the butter and sugar with the syrups, then remove from the heat. Mix 2 tablespoons boiling water with the bicarbonate of soda, then add this to the butter mix. Pour over the oat mixture and stir to combine.

3 Form balls from the mixture using an ice-cream scoop and put on the lined trays, with lots of space around them, about six per tray. Flatten each ball slightly.

4 Bake for 14–16 minutes, depending on how chewy you like them. Allow to stand for 1 minute then transfer to a wire rack to cool.

PER COOKIE 279 kcals, protein 3g, carbs 36g, fat 15g, sat fat 6g, fibre 2g, sugar 20g, salt 0.27g

Clove-sugar cookies

These cookies can be served with after-dinner coffee or packaged up and given as gifts for family and friends. Any leftovers can be stored in your biscuit tin – as if!

TAKES 45 MINUTES • MAKES ABOUT 28

250g/9oz butter, softened
100g/4oz hazelnuts
1 tsp vanilla extract
250g/9oz icing sugar
1½ tsp ground cloves
350g/12oz plain flour

1 Put the butter, hazelnuts, vanilla extract and 85g/3oz of the icing sugar in a food processor and whizz to a paste. Add 1 teaspoon of the ground cloves and all the flour, and pulse together until a dough forms.

2 Heat oven to 200C/180C fan/gas 6. Line a couple of baking sheets with baking parchment. Roll the dough into walnut-size balls and arrange on the baking sheets. Use the back of a fork to lightly squash each ball, then bake for 12–15 minutes until they turn a pale biscuit colour – if they get too brown, they will become dry.

3 Mix the remaining icing sugar and ground cloves, then sieve thickly over the hot biscuits. Leave to cool slightly before eating just warm, or allow to cool.

PER COOKIE 168 kcals, protein 2g, carbs 19g, fat 10g, sat fat 5g, fibre 1g, sugar 10g, salt 0.11g

Toffee–nut squares

It's really worth making a double batch of these moreish little squares as one batch definitely won't be enough!

TAKES 1 HOUR ● MAKES 12, EASILY DOUBLED

25g/1oz pumpkin seeds, plus a few extra to scatter

250g/9oz mixed nuts (we used pistachio nuts, macadamias and hazelnuts)

300g/10oz caramel from a can

3 tbsp flour

FOR THE BASE

175g/6oz plain flour

50g/2oz ground rice

85g/3oz golden caster sugar

140g/5oz cold butter, diced

1 tbsp milk

1 Heat oven to 200C/180C fan/gas 6. Line a 21–22cm-square shallow baking tin with baking parchment. For the base, put the flour, ground rice and sugar in a bowl with the butter and rub in until fine crumbs form. Stir in the milk with a cutlery knife. Tip it all into the tin and press down evenly. Bake for 15–20 minutes until golden.

2 Remove the tin and lower oven to 180C/160C fan/gas 4. Mix together the seeds, nuts, caramel and flour. Evenly distribute over the base, scatter with extra seeds, then bake for 8–10 minutes more. Cool in the tin, then cut into squares.

PER SQUARE 410 kcals, protein 7g, carbs 40g, fat 26g, sat fat 8g, fibre 2g, sugar 23g, salt 0.21g

Spicy tree biscuits

Get the kids to help with these – little fingers will find threading them with ribbon much easier than you will!

TAKES 1 HOUR, PLUS CHILLING
- **MAKES 30–40, DEPENDING ON YOUR CUTTERS**

175g/6oz dark muscovado sugar
85g/3oz golden syrup
100g/4oz butter
3 tsp ground ginger
1 tsp ground cinnamon
350g/12oz plain flour, plus extra for dusting
1 large egg, lightly beaten
1 tsp bicarbonate of soda dissolved in 1 tsp water

TO DECORATE
100g/4oz melted white chocolate and edible silver balls

1 Heat the sugar, syrup and butter until melted. Mix the spices and flour in a large bowl. Make a well in the centre and add the melted sugar mix, egg and bicarbonate of soda. Mix well. Cover the surface of the mix with cling film, cool, then chill for at least 1 hour to become firm.

2 Heat oven to 190C/170C fan/gas 5. Briefly knead the dough then thinly roll out, half at a time, on a floured surface. Cut into shapes with cutters and transfer to baking sheets, leaving room to spread.

3 Bake for 12–15 minutes until slightly darkened. To hang biscuits up, make a hole in each using a skewer while the biscuits are warm and soft. Cool for a few minutes on baking sheets, then transfer to wire racks to cool completely.

4 Drizzle or pipe melted chocolate on to the cold biscuits, then stick on silver balls. If hung up on the tree, biscuits will be edible for a week, but last longer simply as decorations.

PER BISCUIT (30) 119 kcals, protein 2g, carbs 20g, fat 4g, sat fat 2g, fibre none, sugar 11g, salt 0.18g

Gooseberry & almond streusel squares

Gorgeous gooseberries are at their best here when paired with sweet, crumbly shortcake. A dollop of whipped cream elevates these squares to a teatime treat.

TAKES 1 HOUR 10 MINUTES • CUTS INTO 8 SQUARES

250g/9oz chilled butter, chopped
250g/9oz self-raising flour
120g/4½oz ground almonds
120g/4½oz light muscovado sugar
350g/12oz gooseberries, fresh or frozen
85g/3oz caster sugar, plus extra to dust
50g/2oz flaked almonds

1 Heat oven to 190C/170C fan/gas 5. Line a 27 × 18cm baking tin with baking parchment. Rub the butter into the flour, almonds and sugar to make crumbs, then press two-thirds on to the base and sides of the tin.
2 Toss the gooseberries with the caster sugar, then scatter this over the mix in the tin. Mix the flaked almonds into the remaining crumbs, then scatter over the gooseberries.
3 Bake for 50 minutes–1 hour until golden and the fruit is bubbling around the edges. Dredge with extra caster sugar, then cool in the tin before cutting into squares.

PER SQUARE 589 kcals, protein 8g, carbs 56g, fat 38g, sat fat 17g, fibre 4g, sugar 32g, salt 0.78g

Custard kisses

*Sandwich three biscuits together for an over-the-top show stopper of a biscuit,
or simply two for a classic dunker for a cup of tea.*

TAKES 40 MINUTES, PLUS COOLING
- **MAKES 15–25**

100g/4oz softened butter
140g/5oz icing sugar, sifted, plus
    a little extra to dust
2 tbsp custard powder
few drops yellow food colouring
    (optional)

FOR THE BISCUITS

175g/6oz softened butter
50g/2oz golden caster sugar
50g/2oz icing sugar
2 egg yolks
2 tsp vanilla extract
300g/10oz plain flour, plus extra
    for rolling

1 Heat oven to 200C/180C fan/gas 6.
Make the biscuits by mixing together the
butter, sugars, egg yolks and vanilla with
a wooden spoon until creamy, then mix
in the flour in two batches.
2 Roll out the dough thinly on a floured
surface, then use a standard 30cm ruler
to cut it. Start with the ruler flush to one
side and cut along the length. Repeat
these lengths across the width of the
dough, then do the same from the top
down to make small, even squares.
Transfer to baking sheets and bake for
8–10 minutes until golden. Cool.
3 Beat the butter, icing sugar, custard
powder and a few drops of food
colouring, if you want. Pipe or spread a
little on to a biscuit, then sandwich with
one or two more biscuits. Repeat until all
the biscuits are used, then dust with a
little more icing sugar.

PER BISCUIT (15) 220 kcals, protein 1g,
carbs 20g, fat 16g, sat fat 10g, fibre none,
sugar 18g, salt 0.24g

Chocolate chip cookies

Lighter than a usual cookie, these grown-up treats benefit from a good-quality dark chocolate with 70% cocoa solids.

TAKES ABOUT 40 MINUTES
● MAKES 22

85g/3oz butter
1 tbsp cocoa powder
1 tsp instant coffee granules
85g/3oz light muscovado sugar
25g/1oz golden granulated sugar
1 medium egg, beaten
½ tsp vanilla extract
140g/5oz plain flour
½ tsp bicarbonate of soda
85g/3oz dark chocolate, chopped into
    small pieces

1 Line a couple of baking sheets with baking parchment. Put the butter, cocoa and coffee in a pan then heat gently until the butter has melted. Remove from the heat, stir in both the sugars, then cool.
2 Beat the egg and vanilla into the cooled butter mix. Stir the flour and bicarbonate of soda together. Tip into the butter mix with two-thirds of the chocolate, then gently stir together to combine. Don't overmix. Leave for 10–15 minutes to firm up slightly, ready for shaping. Heat oven to 180C/160C fan/gas 4.
3 Using your hands, shape the mixture into 22 small balls. Lay them on the lined sheets, well apart so they have room to spread (you may have to bake in batches). Press the rest of the chocolate pieces on top of each cookie. Bake for 12 minutes. Leave on the sheets for a couple of minutes, then transfer to a wire rack.

PER COOKIE 97 kcals, protein 1g, carbs 12g, fat 5g, sat fat 3g, fibre 1g, sugar 6g, salt 0.12g

Lemon shortbread

The addition of lemon zest makes a lovely citrusy change to a classic shortbread recipe. Try it with lemon first, then how about orange or lime zest, or even grapefruit?

TAKES 45 MINUTES ● CUTS INTO 8 WEDGES

85g/3oz softened butter, plus extra
   for greasing
50g/2oz caster sugar, plus extra for
   sprinkling
100g/4oz plain flour
zest 1 lemon

1 Heat oven to 180C/160C fan/gas 4. Grease a 15cm-round loose-bottomed sandwich tin.
2 Mix the butter and sugar with a wooden spoon, then stir in the flour and lemon zest and press into the tin. Score into eight wedges, prick all over with a fork and sprinkle with extra sugar.
3 Bake for 20–25 minutes or until pale golden in colour. Cool for 10 minutes, then remove from the tin and finish cooling on a wire rack.

PER WEDGE 143 kcals, protein 1g, carbs 18g, fat 8g, sat fat 5g, fibre none, sugar 9g, salt 0.23g

Apricot, honey & pistachio flapjacks

These will keep in an airtight container for up to 3 days – perfect for slipping into the kids' lunchboxes.

TAKES 1 HOUR • MAKES 16

140g/5oz butter, plus extra for greasing
140g/5oz light soft brown sugar
2 tbsp honey
175g/6oz rolled oats
85g/3oz shelled pistachio nuts, chopped
140g/5oz dried apricots, chopped

1 Heat oven to 160C/140C fan/gas 3. Put the butter, sugar and honey in a small pan, then heat gently until melted. Tip the rolled oats, chopped pistachios and apricots into a mixing bowl. Pour over the melted butter mixture and stir to combine.

2 Tip into a 20cm-square greased and lined baking tin, and push down to flatten the surface. Bake for 35–40 minutes until golden and crisp. Cool in the tin, then slice into 16.

PER FLAPJACK 193 kcals, protein 3g, carbs 22g, fat 11g, sat fat 5g, fibre 2g, sugar 15g, salt 0.13g

Fruity cookies

Even easier than rolling into a log and slicing is dolloping spoonfuls of the mixture straight onto baking sheets – use an ice cream scoop to make things extra easy.

TAKES 45 MINUTES ● MAKES 20

200g/7oz butter
175g/6oz light soft brown sugar
2 tbsp thin-cut marmalade
2 tsp ground mixed spice
1 tsp ground cinnamon
1 tsp ground ginger
175g/6oz porridge oats
200g/7oz self-raising flour, plus extra
    for dusting
2 tsp baking powder
175g/6oz dried fruit – try chopped
    glacé cherries, apricots and sultanas
100g/4oz nuts, chopped – try
    hazelnuts, walnuts or pecan nuts

1 Heat oven to 160C/140C fan/gas 3. Cream the butter and sugar until light and fluffy. Mix the marmalade with 2 tablespoons boiling water. Stir into the creamed mix, then add the spices, oats, flour and baking powder. Mix in the fruit and nuts.

2 Dust your hands and the work surface with flour and roll the dough into a long sausage shape. Cut into 20 discs. Put the discs on a baking sheet lined with baking parchment, spaced out as they will spread. Bake for about 25 minutes until golden brown.

PER COOKIE 236 kcals, protein 4g, carbs 30g, fat 12g, sat fat 6g, fibre 2g, sugar 16g, salt 0.42g

Iced ginger shortcake

These crisp, crumbly shortcakes are perfect with a cup of tea or coffee.
The crystallised ginger isn't necessary but does add a lovely punch of flavour.

TAKES 50 MINUTES ● CUTS INTO 16 SLICES

175g/6oz butter, plus extra for greasing
85g/3oz caster sugar
200g/7oz plain flour, plus extra for
    forming the dough
2 tsp ground ginger

FOR THE ICING AND DECORATION

100g/4oz butter
2 tbsp golden syrup
8 heaped tbsp icing sugar
2 tsp ground ginger
crystallised ginger, roughly chopped,
    to decorate (optional)

1 Heat oven to 160C/140C fan/gas 3. Grease a 20cm-square baking tin. Beat the butter and sugar together until pale and fluffy. Sift in the flour and ginger, then mix together with a round-blade knife.

2 Using lightly floured hands, bring the mixture together to form a dough, then spread it into the tin. Bake for 30 minutes until golden. Remove from the oven and leave to cool.

3 For the icing, melt the butter and syrup in a pan. Remove from the heat, sift in the icing sugar and ginger, then mix until smooth and glossy. Cool until almost cold and beat well again.

4 Spread the icing over the shortcake using a palette knife, decorate with the chopped crystallised ginger and serve cut into slices.

PER SLICE 249 kcals, protein 2g, carbs 31g, fat 14g, sat fat 9g, fibre none, sugar 21g, salt 0.28g

Triple choc & chilli cookies

There's only a subtle chilli 'warmth' to these, but if you're making them for kids too you might want to halve the dough and leave the cayenne pepper out of one half.

TAKES 30 MINUTES ● MAKES 40

225g/8oz butter, softened
100g/4oz caster sugar
175g/6oz dark muscovado sugar
2 large eggs, beaten
2 tsp vanilla extract
300g/10oz plain flour
50g/2oz cocoa powder
1 tsp baking powder
1½ tsp cayenne pepper, or less or more to taste
100g bar dark chilli chocolate, roughly chopped
100g bar white chocolate, roughly chopped
100g bar dark chocolate, roughly chopped
vanilla ice cream, to serve

1 Beat the butter and sugars together until smooth, then mix in the eggs and vanilla. In another bowl, combine the flour, cocoa, a pinch of salt, the baking powder and cayenne pepper, then mix these into the creamed butter and sugars, followed by the chocolate chunks.

2 Heat oven to 180C/160C fan/gas 4. Put dollops of the mixture, about a heaped tablespoon, on baking sheets lined with parchment paper, leaving plenty of space in between for spreading. Bake in batches for 10–12 minutes, depending on how gooey you like them. Allow to cool on the baking sheet for 1 minute, before removing to a wire rack to cool.

PER COOKIE 142 kcals, protein 2g, carbs 17g, fat 8g, sat fat 5g, fibre 1g, sugar 11g, salt 0.20g

Lemon fondant cake

Before icing this decadent cake, transfer it to an upturned bowl on a tray, so its edges overhang. This allows excess icing to drip off the sides.

TAKES 2 HOURS, PLUS COOLING

● **CUTS INTO 10 SLICES**

350g/12oz very soft butter
350g/12oz caster sugar, plus 1 tbsp
250g/9oz self-raising flour
3 large eggs
100g/4oz ground almonds
150g pot natural yogurt
zest and juice 2 lemons
12 tbsp lemon curd
500g pack marzipan
500g/1lb 2oz fondant icing sugar,
    sieved, plus extra for dusting
yellow food colouring
icing roses and leaves to decorate,
    if you like

1 Heat oven to 180C/160C fan/gas 4. Grease and line three 20cm-round tins. Beat together the butter, caster sugar, flour, eggs, almonds, yogurt, lemon zest and half the juice. Divide this between the tins and bake for 20–25 minutes.

2 Mix the remaining lemon juice with 1 tablespoon sugar, poke the cakes with a skewer and drizzle over. Cool in the tins.

3 Sandwich the sponges together with 8 tablespoons of the curd. Brush the rest all over the cake. Roll out the marzipan on an icing sugar-dusted surface until large enough to cover the cake. Lift on to the cake. Trim any excess.

4 Mix enough water into the fondant icing sugar to make a thick icing. Set aside a few tablespoons, then mix some yellow food colouring into the rest. Spoon it over the cake, letting it dribble down the sides until the cake is covered.

5 Put the reserved white icing into a food bag. Snip off the corner, pipe over squiggles and decorate, if you like.

PER SLICE 1,015 kcals, protein 10g, carbs 149g, fat 46g, sat fat 21g, fibre 3g, sugar 125g, salt 0.82g

Chocolate & banana cake

If you love banana bread, you'll love this. It also makes a pretty sturdy loaf – perfect if you're transporting it somewhere for a celebration.

TAKES 1 HOUR 35 MINUTES, PLUS COOLING ● CUTS INTO 8–10 SLICES

100ml/3½fl oz sunflower oil, plus extra to grease
175g/6oz caster sugar
175g/6oz self-raising flour
½ tsp bicarbonate of soda
4 tbsp cocoa powder
200g/7oz milk chocolate, half chopped, half broken into chunks
175g/6oz very ripe bananas
3 medium eggs, 2 separated
50ml/2fl oz milk
100ml/3½fl oz soured cream
handful crunchy dried banana chips, roughly chopped, to scatter

1 Heat oven to 160C/140C fan/gas 3. Grease and line a 900g loaf tin, allowing the paper to come 2cm above the top of the tin. Mix the sugar, flour, bicarbonate of soda, cocoa and chopped chocolate in a large bowl.

2 Mash the bananas and mix with the whole egg plus 2 yolks, the oil and milk. Beat the egg whites until stiff. Quickly stir the wet banana mixture into the dry ingredients. Stir in a quarter of the egg whites to loosen the mixture, then gently fold in the rest. Gently scrape into the tin and bake for 1 hour 10–15 minutes, or until a skewer poked in comes out clean. Cool in the tin.

3 To make the icing, melt the chocolate chunks and soured cream together in a heatproof bowl over a pan of barely simmering water. Chill until spreadable. Remove the cake from the tin, swirl the icing over and scatter with banana chips.

PER SLICE (8) 502 kcals, protein 7g, carbs 63g, fat 27g, sat fat 9g, fibre 2g, sugar 43g, salt 0.51g

Vanilla & pomegranate cake

This cake is so versatile – it's delicious served warm or at room temperature, with cream, yogurt or ice cream.

TAKES 1¼ HOURS, PLUS COOLING

● **CUTS INTO 8–10 SLICES**

200g/7oz butter
200g/7oz caster sugar
3 large eggs
zest 1 lemon plus juice of ½ (use the
    other half for the syrup)
½ tsp vanilla extract
140g/5oz self-raising flour
100g/4oz plain flour

FOR THE SYRUP

juice ½ lemon
2 pomegranates, juice of 1, seeds of 1
    (or 100ml/3½fl oz pomegranate juice
    and 110g pack pomegranate seeds)
85g/3oz caster sugar
½ tsp vanilla extract

1 Heat oven to 160C/140C fan/gas 3. Grease and line a deep 20cm-round loose-bottomed cake tin. Beat the butter and sugar with an electric whisk until pale and creamy. Add the eggs, then the lemon zest and juice and vanilla. Fold in the flours. Transfer to the tin, smooth the top, then bake for 50 minutes until risen and golden.

2 To make the syrup, mix the lemon juice with the pomegranate juice, caster sugar and vanilla, then heat gently until the sugar dissolves. Increase the heat and bubble until syrupy. Remove from the heat and cool slightly, then tip in the pomegranate seeds.

3 Remove the cake from the oven. Allow to cool for a few minutes before poking holes all over it with a skewer and pouring over the pomegranate syrup. Enjoy warm or leave to cool completely in the tin.

PER SLICE 475 kcals, protein 6g, carbs 64g, fat 24g, sat fat 14g, fibre 1g, sugar 42g, salt 0.55g

Cherry & almond Easter cake

This is so simple to make and is a delicious almondy twist on a traditional simnel cake.

TAKES 1 HOUR 40 MINUTES ● CUTS INTO 12 SLICES

250g pack butter, softened, plus extra
    for greasing
175g/6oz golden caster sugar
5 large eggs, beaten
250g/9oz self-raising flour, plus an
    extra 2 tbsp for the cherries
1 tsp baking powder
zest 1 orange, plus 2 tbsp juice
200g/7oz glacé cherries, halved
250g/9oz marzipan, coarsely grated
    (easiest if chilled beforehand)

FOR THE DECORATION

100g/4oz icing sugar, sifted
50g/2oz toasted flaked almonds
12 natural glacé cherries
zest 1 orange

1 Heat oven to 160C/140C fan/gas 3 and grease and line a deep 20cm-round loose-bottomed cake tin. Beat the butter and sugar together with an electric whisk until light and fluffy. Beat in the eggs, flour, baking powder, orange zest and juice.

2 Toss the cherries in the additional 2 tablespoons flour and fold into the batter along with the grated marzipan. Spoon into the tin, level and bake for 1½ hours – a skewer will come out clean when ready. Cool in the tin for about 10 minutes, then finish on a wire rack.

3 Mix the icing sugar with just over 1 tablespoon water to make a loose but not-too-runny icing. Scatter the almonds over the top of the cake and position glacé cherries around the edge, using icing to fix them in place. Drizzle icing over the cake and finish with a scattering of orange zest.

PER SLICE 515 kcals, protein 7g, carbs 69g, fat 25g, sat fat 12g, fibre 2g, sugar 53g, salt 0.76g

Sticky banana & maple cake

This gorgeous sticky cake makes a lovely pudding with ice cream or crème fraîche and plenty more maple syrup on the side.

TAKES 1½ HOURS • SERVES 8

100g/4oz softened butter, plus extra
    for greasing
8 tbsp maple syrup, plus extra to serve
3 small ripe bananas and 1 over-ripe
    banana
200g/7oz light muscovado sugar
4 large eggs
2 tsp vanilla paste or seeds scraped
    from 2 vanilla pods
200g/7oz self-raising flour
100g/4oz ground almonds
1 tsp bicarbonate of soda
200g pot Greek yogurt

1 Heat oven to 160C/140C fan/gas 3, then butter and line the base of a deep 20cm-square cake tin. Pour in half the syrup, swirling to coat the bottom. Halve the 3 ripe bananas lengthways and lay, cut-side down, in the tin.

2 Beat together the butter, sugar, eggs, vanilla and over-ripe banana with an electric whisk. Fold in the flour, almonds and bicarbonate of soda, then stir in the yogurt. Carefully spoon into the tin without dislodging the bananas. Bake for 45 minutes–1 hour until a skewer poked in comes out with only moist crumbs.

3 Poke all over with the skewer, then pour over the remaining maple syrup. Let it soak in for a few minutes, then carefully turn the cake out of the tin upside-down, drizzling the banana-studded top with more syrup. Slice and serve warm.

PER SERVING 514 kcals, protein 11g, carbs 68g, fat 24g, sat fat 10g, fibre 2g, sugar 47g, salt 1g

Double-the-love chocolate cake

This can easily be made a day ahead, and by baking the sponges in batches, you need only two tins. A simple white buttercream looks great swirled over, however roughly.

TAKES 4 HOURS, PLUS COOLING

● **SERVES 25**

2 × 200g bars white chocolate, melted and cooled a bit

550g/1lb 4oz very soft butter (but not melted)

550g/1lb 4oz icing sugar

2–3 × 80g bags white chocolate buttons

FOR THE SPONGES

400g/14oz butter

200g/7oz plain chocolate

700g/1lb 8oz plain flour

800g/1lb 12oz caster sugar

100g/4oz cocoa powder

2 tsp bicarbonate of soda

4 large eggs

400ml/14fl oz buttermilk

150ml/¼ pint boiling water

1 Heat oven to 180C/160C fan/gas 4. Grease and generously line a deep 20cm-round cake tin and a 15cm one.
2 Gently melt half the butter and half the chocolate for the sponges in a pan. Mix half of the dry sponge ingredients with ¼ teaspoon salt. Whisk 2 eggs with 200ml/7fl oz buttermilk. Add the chocolate and egg mixtures to the dry ingredients with the boiling water. Beat with an electric whisk until lump-free. Divide between the tins and bake for 40–45 minutes (the 15cm cake should take 40 minutes). Cool in the tins.
3 Repeat the steps, so you end up with two 20cm and two 15cm cakes.
4 Stir together the melted white chocolate, butter and icing sugar. Halve each cooled cake. Sandwich matching halves with icing to get two four-layered cakes. Sit a 20cm cake on your serving plate and spread icing over the top. Sit the smaller cake on top, and completely cover with icing and chocolate buttons.

PER SERVING 729 kcals, protein 7g, carbs 83g, fat 43g, sat fat 26g, fibre 2g, sugar 60g, salt 0.79g

Frosted courgette & lemon cake

Don't be put off by the courgette – it adds moistness, colour and a lovely mellow note to this delicious cake.

TAKES 45 MINUTES, PLUS COOLING

● **CUTS INTO 12 SLICES**

250g pack unsalted butter, very soft, plus extra for the tin

200g/7oz golden caster sugar

3 large eggs

1 tsp poppy seeds, plus extra to decorate

2 medium courgettes, coarsely grated (you'll need 300g/10oz flesh)

1 tsp vanilla extract

zest 3 lemons, juice 2

100g/4oz each self-raising flour and plain wholemeal flour

1 tsp baking powder

85g/3oz icing sugar

200g pack full-fat soft cheese

4 tbsp lemon curd

1 Heat oven to 180C/160C fan/gas 4. Butter and line the bases of two 20cm sandwich tins. Beat 200g/7oz of the butter, the caster sugar, eggs, poppy seeds, courgettes, vanilla and two-thirds of the zest together. Stir in 1 tablespoon of the lemon juice, the flours, baking powder and ¼ teaspoon salt. Spoon into the tins, then bake for 25 minutes.

2 Mix 1 tablespoon of the lemon juice with 25g/1oz of the icing sugar. When the cakes are done, cool for 15 minutes in the tins, then turn on to wire racks set over a tray. Prick the cakes several times with a cocktail stick, spoon over the lemon drizzle and leave to cool.

3 Beat the remaining icing sugar and butter, the soft cheese, remaining lemon juice and zest to a smooth frosting. Spread one cake with just under half the frosting and spread over the curd. Top with the second cake, spread the remaining frosting over the top and sprinkle with poppy seeds.

PER SLICE 375 kcals, protein 7g, carbs 38g, fat 23g, sat fat 14g, fibre 1g, sugar 26g, salt 0.68g

Summer-fruit drizzle cake

Try making this cake with any berries but strawberries, just experiment to suit your mood – or your fruitbowl!

TAKES 1¼ HOURS • CUTS INTO 8 SLICES

175g/6oz very soft butter, plus extra
    for greasing
175g/6oz golden caster sugar
250g/9oz self-raising flour
2 large eggs
2 tsp vanilla extract
175g/6oz mixed raspberries and
    blackberries, chopped if large
140g/5oz granulated sugar
1–2 tbsp lemon juice

1 Heat oven to 180C/160C fan/gas 4. Grease and line the base and ends of a 900g loaf tin. Put the butter, caster sugar, flour, eggs and vanilla into a large bowl and beat with an electric whisk for 5 minutes until pale and creamy – the mixture will be very thick.

2 Spread one-third of the cake mix into the tin, then scatter over 50g/2oz of the fruit. Spread another third of the cake mix on top, and scatter with another 50g/2oz fruit. Finally, dot the remaining cake mix over and spread. Bake for 1 hour, until an inserted skewer comes out clean.

3 Poke the cake all over with a skewer. Put the remaining fruit into a bowl with the granulated sugar. Stir in 1 tablespoon lemon juice first with a fork, mashing a little of the fruit as you go (if it's a bit dry, add a splash more juice), then spoon over the cake. Leave in the tin until the cake is cool and the topping is set.

PER SERVING 457 kcals, protein 5g, carbs 67g, fat 21g, sat fat 12g, fibre 1g, sugar 44g, salt 0.62g

Pear & mincemeat crumble cake

With a hint of spice and little pockets of mincemeat, this is a lovely post-Christmas cake. Great served warm with custard, too.

TAKES 2 HOURS, PLUS COOLING
- **CUTS INTO 12 SLICES**

4 firm pears, peeled, cored and cut into thumb-size chunks
3 tbsp golden caster sugar
1 tsp ground mixed spice

FOR THE CAKE MIX

250g pack salted butter, softened, plus extra for greasing
250g/9oz golden caster sugar
1 tsp vanilla extract or paste
5 large eggs
200g/7oz self-raising flour
100g/4oz ground almonds
7 tbsp plain flour
6 tbsp mincemeat

1 Put the pears into a non-stick frying pan with 2 tablespoons of the sugar and 2 tablespoons water. Cover and cook for 10 minutes, stirring often. Tip off any juices, add the spice and leave to cool.

2 Heat oven to 160C/140C fan/gas 3. Butter then line a deep 20cm-round cake tin. Beat the butter, sugar, vanilla and ¼ teaspoon salt until pale and fluffy. Add the eggs and self-raising flour, beat until smooth, then fold in the almonds.

3 Remove 85g/3oz batter and to this add the plain flour and chop it into the mix with a cutlery knife.

4 Spoon half the cake mix into the tin, top with half the pears, dot over half the mincemeat, then dollop the rest of the cake mix on top. Scatter with the remaining pears and mincemeat, then the crumble mix. Sprinkle with the final 1 tablespoon sugar. Bake for 1½ hours, covering with foil after 1 hour, until cooked. Cool in the tin for 10 minutes.

PER SLICE 442 kcals, protein 7g, carbs 50g, fat 25g, sat fat 12g, fibre 2g, sugar 36g, salt 0.56g

Sticky-citrus sponge cake

Make this for Sunday lunch and your family will love you for ever – delicious warm or cold.

TAKES 1 HOUR 10 MINUTES • CUTS INTO 10 SLICES

4 medium oranges
6 tbsp golden syrup, plus extra to drizzle (optional)
200g/7oz butter, at room temperature, plus extra for greasing
200g/7oz soft brown sugar
200g/7oz self-raising flour
1 tsp baking powder
100g/4oz ground almonds
4 large eggs

1 Heat oven to 180C/160C fan/gas 4. Finely grate the zest from two oranges into a large bowl. Cut the peel and pith from all the oranges with a serrated knife, and slice quite thickly.
2 Drizzle the golden syrup evenly over the base of a greased 23cm-round cake tin. (There is no need to line the tin and it shouldn't have a loose bottom otherwise the syrup will bubble through.) Arrange the best orange slices on top of the syrup and finely chop any that don't fit.
3 Put all the remaining ingredients in the bowl with the zest and chopped orange. Beat with an electric hand mixer until smooth. Spoon on top of the oranges, spread lightly and make a deep hollow in the centre of the mix with a spoon.
4 Bake for 45–50 minutes until firm when pressed. Allow to settle for 5 minutes before turning out. Drizzle with extra golden syrup, if you like, and serve with custard or ice cream.

PER SLICE 442 kcals, protein 8g, carbs 49g, fat 25g, sat fat 12g, fibre 2g, sugar 33g, salt 0.73g

Chocolate-fudge birthday cake

Decorate this cake however you want to – the more sweets, the better!

TAKES 1½ HOURS, PLUS COOLING

● **CUTS INTO 8–10 SLICES**

250g/9oz plain flour

1½ tsp each baking powder and
   bicarbonate of soda

3 tbsp cocoa powder

140g/5oz dark chocolate, broken into
   chunks

100ml/3½fl oz water, hand hot

175g/6oz butter, softened

250g/9oz caster sugar

3 large eggs

200g/7oz full-fat natural yogurt

100ml/3½fl oz double cream

50g/2oz milk chocolate, broken into
   chunks

sweets, to decorate

1 Heat oven to 160C/140C fan/ gas 3. Grease and line a 22cm-round cake tin.

2 Sift the flour, baking powder, cocoa and bicarbonate of soda into a bowl.

3 Put 100g/4oz of the dark chocolate in a heatproof bowl and pour over the water. Leave for 1 minute, then stir until the mixture is smooth and melted.

4 Beat the butter and sugar until creamy, then beat in the eggs. Pour in the melted chocolate and mix. Spoon in the yogurt and the flour mixture, and mix well.

5 Spread the mixture evenly in the tin and bake for 55 minutes until an inserted skewer comes out clean. Cool in the tin.

6 For the icing, heat the cream in a pan to just below boiling. Remove from heat and stir in the remaining dark and the milk chocolate. Cool until thick.

7 Set the cake upside-down on a serving plate. Spread the icing on the top and sides of the cake to cover completely. Decorate, then leave somewhere cool (not the fridge) to firm up.

PER SLICE 653 kcals, protein 10g, carbs 70g, fat 37g, sat fat 22g, fibre 2g, sugar 48g, salt 0.90g

Eton mess cake

Buy a 300ml tub of double cream and you'll have enough left to serve with this very British cake.

TAKES 1 HOUR 10 MINUTES • CUTS INTO 15 SLICES

175g/6oz unsalted butter, plus extra for greasing
5 tbsp double cream
1 tsp vanilla paste or extract
225g/8oz plain flour
100g/4oz ground almonds
1 tsp baking powder
200g/7oz golden caster sugar
5 large eggs
400g/14oz strawberries, half roughly chopped, half finely sliced
4 meringue nests (50g/2oz), very roughly broken up
a little icing sugar, to dust

1 Grease a deep 20 × 30cm traybake or roasting tin. Heat oven to 160C/140C fan/gas 3. Melt the butter, take off the heat and stir in the cream and the vanilla. Mix the flour, almonds, baking powder and ¼ teaspoon fine salt.
2 Put the caster sugar and eggs into a large bowl, and whisk with an electric whisk until very thick and foamy, about 5 minutes. Pour in the butter mix, whisk briefly, then add the flour mix and whisk briefly again until even. Stir in the chopped strawberries, then pour the batter into the tin and level the top.
3 Scatter the sliced strawberries and meringue over the cake, then bake for 40–45 minutes until risen, golden and a skewer comes out clean. Cool for 20 minutes in the tin, then turn out on to a wire rack. Just before serving, dust with a little icing sugar.

PER SLICE 306 kcals, protein 6g, carbs 31g, fat 18g, sat fat 9g, fibre 1g, sugar 20g, salt 0.17g

Little rose & almond cupcakes

Stamping out circles of icing and marzipan is the easiest way to give cupcakes a really smart look – and these clever spiral roses actually look better the less neat they are!

**TAKES 2 HOURS ● MAKES 12,
EASILY DOUBLED**

FOR THE CAKE

140g/5oz self-raising flour
100g/4oz ground almonds
½ tsp baking powder
175g/6oz caster sugar
½ tsp almond extract
3 large eggs
100g/4oz natural yogurt
175g/6oz melted butter

TO DECORATE

175g/6oz marzipan
100g/4oz icing sugar, plus extra for
    dusting and sticking syrup
350g/12oz ready-roll icing
yellow, pink and green food colourings

1 Heat oven to 180C/160C fan/gas 4. Line a 12-hole muffin tin with cases. Beat the cake ingredients together until smooth. Divide among the cases and bake for 18–22 minutes. Cool on a wire rack.
2 Roll out the marzipan on an icing sugar-dusted surface to £1 coin thickness. Using a 6cm cutter, stamp out 12 circles. Mix some icing sugar and water to give a syrupy icing, then brush over the backs of the marzipan and stick on to the cakes.
3 Knead a little yellow food colouring into one quarter of the ready-roll icing, pink into another quarter and green into another quarter. Repeat step 2 using a 7cm cutter to stamp out four circles each from the pink, yellow and white icing, sticking again with syrupy icing.
4 Make a stiff-ish icing with the 100g/4oz icing sugar. Divide into three, leave one white and colour the others pink and yellow. Pipe in spirals on the cakes. Pinch small bits of green icing into leaves and stick on using the syrupy icing.

PER CUPCAKE 488 kcals, protein 6g, carbs 72g, fat 22g, sat fat 9g, fibre 1g, sugar 63g, salt 0.46g

Eccles cake

Christmas, bake sales, birthdays with ice cream – this seems to go down well on any occasion!

TAKES 2 HOURS ● CUTS INTO 8–10 SLICES

FOR SPONGE MIXTURE

250g pack butter, softened
250g/9oz light soft brown sugar
2 tsp vanilla extract
4 large eggs
100g/4oz plain flour
250g/9oz self-raising flour
100g/4oz buttermilk
2 eating apples, peeled, cored and
  diced

FOR THE FILLING

1 tsp each ground cinnamon and mixed
  spice
2 tbsp each melted butter and light
  soft brown sugar
85g/3oz each currants and raisins
50g/2oz mixed peel

TO DECORATE

85g/3oz icing sugar, sifted
zest and juice 1 lemon
few sugar cubes, roughly crushed

1 Heat oven to 160C/140C fan/gas 3. Grease and line a deep 20cm-round cake tin. Mix the filling ingredients together.
2 Beat all the sponge ingredients, apart from the apples, with an electric whisk until smooth. Fold in the diced apples. Scrape half the mixture into the tin, then scatter over the filling, leaving a 2.5cm clear border all round the edge. Spoon the remaining sponge batter on top – start by dolloping round the edges, then move into the middle. Bake for 1 hour 25 minutes. Cool in the tin.
3 To finish, mix the icing sugar with enough lemon juice for a runny-ish icing. Drizzle over the cake and scatter with the crushed sugar and lemon zest.

PER SLICE 571 kcals, protein 7g, carbs 76g, fat 27g, sat fat 16g, fibre 2g, sugar 53g, salt 0.80g

Red velvet cake

If you don't like using artificial food colouring, we've added some beetroot to this gorgeous squidgy cake, so even without it you'll have a little hue to the sponges.

TAKES 1½ HOURS, PLUS COOLING

● **CUTS INTO 12 SLICES**

FOR THE SPONGES

250g/9oz butter, plus extra for greasing

200g/7oz dark chocolate, broken into chunks

500g/18oz each plain flour and golden caster sugar

2 tbsp cocoa powder

1 tsp bicarbonate of soda

2 large eggs

200g/7oz natural yogurt

400g/14oz cooked beetroot – don't use the ones dipped in vinegar!

4 tbsp artificial red food colouring, or 2 × 28ml bottles

300ml/10fl oz boiling water

TO FINISH

200g pack full-fat cream cheese (out of the fridge for 30 minutes)

250g pack butter, softened

400g/14oz icing sugar, sifted

2 tsp vanilla extract

few sweets, to decorate

1 Heat oven to 180C/160C fan/gas 4. Grease and line the base and sides of two 20cm-round tins. Gently melt half the butter and half the chocolate together. Mix half of all the flour, sugar, cocoa and bicarbonate of soda with ¼ teaspoon salt. Whizz 1 egg, half the yogurt and half the beetroot in a food processor until smooth-ish.

2 Stir the beetroot and chocolate mixes into the dry ingredients with half the food colouring and half the boiling water. Divide the mixture between the tins. Bake for 25 minutes until a skewer poked in comes out clean. Cool the cake.

3 Repeat steps 1 and 2 with the remaining sponge ingredients.

4 Briefly beat together the cream cheese, butter, icing sugar and vanilla. Use a little of this to sandwich the four cooled cakes together, then swirl the rest all over the outside and decorate with sweets.

PER SLICE 656 kcals, protein 5g, carbs 75g, fat 37g, sat fat 23g, fibre 1g, sugar 61g, salt 0.80g

Rich fruit Christmas cake

This traditional fruit cake is gluten free so everyone can enjoy it on Christmas Day – or whenever you want to make it!

TAKES 2 HOURS, PLUS OVERNIGHT SOAKING AND COOLING ● MAKES AN 18CM CAKE

500g/1lb 2oz luxury mixed dried fruits (check gluten-free)
150ml/¼ pint whisky
zest and juice 1 lemon
140g/5oz butter, softened, plus extra for greasing
140g/5oz dark soft brown sugar
3 medium eggs
140g/5oz gluten-free flour
1 tsp each gluten-free baking powder and xanthan gum
1 tsp each ground mixed spice and ground allspice
50g/2oz ground almonds
2 tbsp each milk and honey

FOR THE DECORATION

2 tbsp smooth apricot jam, warmed
100g/4oz mixed glacé fruits and whole nuts

1 Bring the dried fruit, whisky, lemon zest and juice to the boil in a pan. Remove from the heat, cover and soak overnight.

2 Heat oven to 150C/130C fan/gas 2. Grease and line the base and sides of a very deep 18cm-round cake tin. Beat the butter and sugar in a big bowl until light and fluffy. Beat in the eggs, then stir in the flour, baking powder, xanthan gum, spices, almonds, milk, honey and soaked fruit and juices. Spoon into the tin and bake for 1½–2 hours or until a skewer inserted into the centre comes out clean. Cool in the tin.

3 To decorate, brush the top of the cake with half the jam. Arrange glacé fruits and nuts on top and brush over more jam.

PER SLICE 557 kcals, protein 6g, carbs 80g, fat 20g, sat fat 8g, fibre 3g, sugar 69g, salt 0.50g

Apple & walnut cake with treacle icing

Golden syrup works just as well as treacle here, if you'd like a lighter flavour.

**TAKES 1 HOUR 20 MINUTES, PLUS
COOLING • CUTS INTO 10 SLICES**

300g/10oz plain flour
1 tsp ground cinnamon
½ tsp bicarbonate of soda
140g/5oz dark soft brown sugar, sieved
50g/2oz golden caster sugar
250ml/9fl oz rapeseed or sunflower oil,
    plus extra for greasing
4 large eggs
3 unpeeled apples, coarsely grated
100g/4oz walnuts, roughly chopped

FOR THE ICING

100g/4oz butter, softened
50g/2oz dark soft brown sugar
1 tbsp black treacle
200g tub full-fat soft cheese

1 Heat oven to 150C/130C fan/gas 2. Grease and line two 20cm-round cake tins. Mix the flour, cinnamon, bicarbonate of soda and sugars in a big bowl. Stir in the oil, eggs and apples, and fold in the walnuts. Divide between the tins and bake for 45 minutes or until a skewer comes out clean. Cool for a few minutes in the tin then cool on wire racks.

2 Beat all the icing ingredients together then chill until thick but spreadable. Spread the icing over the top of each cake and sandwich together.

PER SLICE 535 kcals, protein 15g, carbs 89g, fat 14g, sat fat 8g, fibre 2g, sugar 51g, salt 0.46g

Cranberry & cream cheese muffins

These unusual muffins are perfect for Christmas morning: a little tart, a little sweet, and perfect with the first coffee of the day.

TAKES 40 MINUTES PLUS COOLING
- **MAKES 12**

100g/4oz full-fat soft cheese
250g/9oz caster sugar
175g/6oz cranberries (frozen or fresh)
200g/7oz plain flour
2 tsp baking powder
2 large eggs
75ml/2½fl oz flavourless oil, such as
    sunflower
1 tsp vanilla extract

1 Heat oven to 190C/170C fan/gas 5. Line a 12-hole muffin tin with muffin cases. Beat the soft cheese with 25g/1oz of the sugar and chill until needed. Heat the cranberries together with another 25g/1oz of sugar until they start to pop. Mash lightly and set aside to cool.

2 Sift the flour into a large bowl and add the remaining sugar, the baking powder and a pinch of salt. Add the eggs, oil, vanilla and cranberry mixture, and stir together – don't worry if it looks a bit lumpy. Divide the mix between the cases, they should look about two-thirds full. Make a small dip in the centre of each and put in a blob of soft cheese. Bake for 25 minutes or until risen and golden. Cool on a wire rack.

PER MUFFIN 230 kcals, protein 3g, carbs 36g, fat 9g, sat fat 2g, fibre 1g, sugar 23g, salt 0.33g

Pistachio & milk chocolate squares

If you've got the girls over for a glamorous get-together, these are the ideal treats to serve on something pretty – just add cake forks to avoid sticky fingers!

TAKES 1 HOUR 20 MINUTES, PLUS COOLING • CUTS INTO 16 SQUARES

140g/5oz shelled pistachio nuts
200g/7oz milk chocolate, broken into chunks
200g/7oz golden caster sugar
200g/7oz very soft butter
3 large eggs
200g/7oz self-raising flour
100ml/3½fl oz milk
150ml/¼ pint soured cream

1 Heat oven to 180C/160C fan/gas 4. Line a 20cm-square cake tin with baking parchment. Whizz 125g/4½oz of the pistachios, 75g/2¾oz of the chocolate and about half the sugar in a food processor until very finely chopped.
2 Tip into a bowl with the remaining sugar, the butter, eggs, flour and milk, plus a pinch of salt, and beat. Scrape into the tin and bake for 35–45 minutes until a skewer poked in comes out clean. Cool.
3 Melt the remaining milk chocolate in a bowl set over a pan of gently simmering water. Take off the heat, stir in the soured cream and cool until spreadable.
4 Trim the edges off the cake, then split in half. Spread a little icing over the base and sandwich the top of sponge back on. Spread the remaining icing over the top, then roughly chop the remaining pistachios and scatter them over. Cut into 16 squares to serve.

PER SQUARE 342 kcals, protein 6g, carbs 32g, fat 22g, sat fat 11g, fibre 1g, sugar 22g, salt 0.35g

Selkirk bannok

A deliciously simple yeasted bread studded with sultanas. This is a classic that should be served with plenty of butter. If you have any left over, toast it for breakfast.

TAKES 1 HOUR 10 MINUTES, PLUS RISING ● MAKES 1 LARGE LOAF, ENOUGH FOR 8

7g sachet fast-action yeast
1 tsp caster sugar
500g/1lb 2oz strong white flour
140g/5oz unsalted butter, melted and cooled
oil, for greasing
450g/1lb sultanas
50g/2oz light brown sugar
milk for glazing

1 In a large bowl, mix the yeast and caster sugar with 250ml/9fl oz warm water. Let it stand for 10 minutes until the mixture becomes frothy. Tip in the flour and 125g/4½oz of the butter and mix to form a smooth, soft dough. Knead for 5 minutes, then put the mixture back in the bowl. Cover with oiled cling film and leave to rise in a warm place until doubled in size.

2 Knead the dough lightly for 1 minute, then knead in the sultanas and brown sugar. Grease a deep 23cm-round cake tin with the remaining butter. Shape the dough into a round and put it in the tin. Cover with oiled cling film and leave to rise again until doubled in size.

3 Heat oven to 180C/160C fan/gas 4. Brush the bannok with a little milk, then bake for 45–50 minutes until risen and browned. The bread should sound hollow when removed from the tin and the base is tapped. Cool on a wire rack.

PER SERVING 525 kcals, protein 9g, carbs 93g, fat 16g, sat fat 9g, fibre 3g, sugar 47g, salt 0.04g

Spiced toffee apple cake

This cake is a twist on traditional toffee apples. Enjoy with a cuppa, or warm with cream and extra toffee sauce – yummy!

TAKES 2 HOURS, PLUS COOLING

● CUTS INTO 15 SQUARES

200g/7oz dates, roughly chopped
200ml/7fl oz milk, plus a splash
250g pack butter, softened
300g/10oz self-raising flour
200g/7oz light soft brown sugar
½ tsp baking powder
4 large eggs
1 tbsp ground mixed spice
2 tsp vanilla extract
3 small red apples
squeeze lemon juice

TO FINISH

handful of toffees and a little icing sugar

1 Heat oven to 180C/160C fan/gas 4. Line a 20 × 30cm baking tin. Bring the dates and milk to a simmer in a pan, then cool for 15 minutes.

2 Whizz the date mixture to a smooth purée in a food processor or blender, then scrape into a large mixing bowl. Add the butter, flour, brown sugar, baking powder, eggs, mixed spice and vanilla.

3 Quarter, core and thinly slice the apples, tossing in lemon juice as you go.

4 Beat together the cake ingredients with an electric whisk. Scrape into the baking tin and arrange the apple slices, overlapping in rows, on top. Bake for 45–50 minutes until a skewer poked into the centre of the cake comes out clean. Cool in the tin.

5 Put the toffees in a small pan with a good splash of milk and gently melt, stirring. Dust the cake with icing sugar, drizzle over the sauce, then cut into squares to serve.

PER SQUARE 327 kcals, protein 5g, carbs 42g, fat 17g, sat fat 10g, fibre 2g, sugar 27g, salt 0.53g

Queen of pudding cakes

Inspired by the popular British dessert, Queen of Puddings, these cakes look very cute and fancy but are dead easy. You can find mini meringues in supermarkets.

TAKES 40 MINUTES, PLUS COOLING

● **CUTS INTO 16 SQUARES**

200g/7oz soft butter, plus extra for greasing
200g/7oz golden caster sugar
3 large eggs
140g/5oz self-raising flour
50g/2oz custard powder
5–6 tbsp raspberry jam
16 mini meringues
icing sugar, to dust (optional)

1 Heat oven to 180C/160C fan/gas 4. Grease and line a 20cm-square baking tin. Whisk together the butter, sugar, eggs, flour and custard powder until well combined and fluffy. Spread into the tin and bake for 25–30 minutes until golden and risen. Cool in the tin.

2 Remove the cooled cake from the tin and spread with the jam. Trim the edges, then cut into 16 squares. Just before serving, add a meringue to each square and dust with icing sugar, if you like.

PER SQUARE 232 kcals, protein 3g, carbs 31g, fat 12g, sat fat 7g, fibre none, sugar 22g, salt 0.32g

Chocolate & hazelnut brownies

You can cut these brownies as big or as small as you want them – but we think big is better!

TAKES 1 HOUR ● **CUTS INTO 9 SQUARES**

100g/4oz dark chocolate, broken into chunks

100g/4oz milk chocolate, broken into chunks

85g/3oz butter

100g/4oz light muscovado sugar

85g/3oz dark muscovado sugar

3 large eggs, beaten with a fork

140g/5oz plain flour

100g/4oz hazelnuts, roughly chopped

1 Heat oven to 180C/160C fan/gas 6 and line the base of a shallow 20cm-square baking tin. Melt the chocolates and butter in a heatproof bowl set over a pan of simmering water. Remove from the heat, then stir in the sugars. Cool a little while you prepare the rest of the ingredients.

2 Stir the eggs into the chocolate mixture, followed by the flour, most of the hazelnuts and a pinch of salt until really well combined. Pour the mixture into the prepared tin, scatter with the remaining hazelnuts, then bake for 25–30 minutes until an inserted skewer comes out with sticky crumbs. Cool in the tin.

3 To serve, cut the brownies into chunks.

PER SQUARE 413 kcals, protein 7g, carbs 44g, fat 23g, sat fat 10g, fibre 2g, sugar 33g, salt 0.20g

Little ginger loaf cakes

You'll find card or paper mini-loaf cases in kitchen and baking shops, and even some supermarkets, or look online at baking websites.

**TAKES 50 MINUTES • MAKES
10 MINI CAKES**

120g/4½oz butter, cut into cubes, plus
    extra for greasing
225g/8oz self-raising flour
1 tsp each bicarbonate of soda, ground
    cinnamon and mixed spice
1 tbsp ground ginger
120g/4½oz dark muscovado sugar
120g/4½oz each black treacle and
    golden syrup
250ml/9fl oz full-fat milk
85g/3oz drained stem ginger, finely
    grated
1 large egg

TO ICE AND DECORATE

50g/2oz icing sugar, sifted
1 tsp finely grated lemon zest and
    2 tsp lemon juice
few chunks crystallised ginger,
    chopped

1 Heat oven to 180C/160C fan/gas 4. Grease and line ten mini loaf tins (or use card ones). Put the butter, flour, bicarbonate of soda and spices into a large mixing bowl. Rub in the butter with your fingertips.

2 Melt the sugar, treacle, syrup and milk in a pan, stirring, then bring the mixture to just below boiling point.

3 Add the stem ginger to the flour mixture, then stir in the treacle mixture. Beat in the egg then spoon the mixture into the tins to about half or three-quarters full. Bake for 16–18 minutes, until a skewer pushed into the centre of a cake comes out clean. Cool.

4 To make the icing, mix the icing sugar and lemon zest, then gradually add the lemon juice to make a smooth, slightly runny icing. Spoon a little on each cake and add some crystallised ginger to finish.

PER CAKE 355 kcals, protein 4g, carbs 58g, fat 12g, sat fat 7g, fibre 1g, sugar 42g, salt 0.90g

Pistachio cupcakes

These pretty little cakes will add wow factor to any get-together, and best of all they are so easy to decorate – not a piping bag in sight!

TAKES 50 MINUTES, PLUS COOLING

● **MAKES 12**

100g/4oz pistachio nuts
140g/5oz golden caster sugar
140g/5oz butter, very soft
2 large eggs
140g/5oz self-raising flour
5 tbsp milk

TO ICE AND DECORATE

250g/9oz fondant icing sugar, sifted
mint green food colouring and edible
   glitter (optional)

1 Heat oven to 160C/140C fan/gas 3 and line a 12-hole muffin tin with cases. Put 85g/3oz of the pistachios into a food processor with roughly half the sugar, then whizz until finely chopped. Tip into a large mixing bowl with the remaining sugar, butter, eggs, flour and milk, and beat until smooth. Divide the mix among the cases, then bake on a low shelf for 22–25 minutes until a skewer poked in comes out clean. Cool on a wire rack.

2 Gradually mix enough water into the icing sugar to get a thick but still runny icing. Stir in drops of food colouring, if you wish, to give a pale colour. If any cake pokes above the top of the case, scoop out with a teaspoon – being careful not to release the case from the sides of the cake. Put a spoonful of icing on each cake and let it spread to cover. Chop the remaining pistachios and scatter these over with a pinch of edible glitter too, if you like. Leave to set, then serve.

PER CUPCAKE 326 kcals, protein 4g, carbs 45g, fat 16g, sat fat 7g, fibre none, sugar 36g, salt 0.34g

Hazelnut fruitcake

The timing for this cake can depend on the water content of the courgettes, so return it to the oven if needed. Simply test with a skewer and make sure it comes out clean.

TAKES 1 HOUR 50 MINUTES • CUTS INTO 10 SLICES

225g/8oz soft unsalted butter, plus a little extra for greasing

100g bag blanched hazelnuts, half very roughly chopped

225g/8oz light muscovado sugar

225g/8oz self-raising flour

3 large eggs

1 tsp vanilla extract

2 tsp ground mixed spice or cinnamon

1 tsp baking powder

175g/6oz courgettes, coarsely grated

1 eating apple, grated (about 85g/3oz flesh)

250g/9oz mixed dried fruit

1 Heat oven to 180C/160C fan/gas 4. Grease and line a deep 20cm-round cake tin. Put the whole hazelnuts, plus 1 tablespoon each of the sugar and flour, into a food processor and whizz until the hazelnuts are as fine as you can get them.

2 Add the butter, the remaining sugar and flour, the eggs, vanilla, spice, ¼ teaspoon salt and the baking powder to the processor. Whizz until smooth. Remove the blade, then stir in the grated courgettes, apple and dried fruit.

3 Spoon the mix into the tin, smooth the top, then scatter with the chopped hazelnuts. Bake for 1 hour 10 minutes, covering the top loosely with foil after 45 minutes, until the cake is risen and golden. Cool in the tin for 20 minutes, then turn out on to a wire rack to cool.

PER SLICE 501 kcals, protein 7g, carbs 59g, fat 28g, sat fat 13g, fibre 2g, sugar 42g, salt 0.87g

Cappuccino cake

Creamy white icing, dusted with cocoa, all sitting on top of a light, coffee sponge – all the layers of a classic cappuccino!

TAKES 55 MINUTES, PLUS COOLING
● **CUTS INTO 15 SQUARES**

250g/9oz softened butter, plus extra
    for greasing
300g/10oz self-raising flour
250g/9oz golden caster sugar
½ tsp baking powder
4 large eggs
150g pot natural yogurt
1 tsp vanilla paste or extract
1 tbsp cocoa powder, plus extra to dust
100ml/3½fl oz strong coffee (we made
    it with 2 tbsp coffee granules)
140g/5oz icing sugar, sifted
350g/12oz mascarpone or full-fat soft
    cheese
few chocolate-covered coffee beans,
    to decorate

1 Heat oven to 180C/160C fan/gas 4. Grease and line a 20 × 30cm baking or roasting tin. Beat the butter, flour, sugar, baking powder, eggs, yogurt, vanilla, cocoa and half the coffee in a large bowl with an electric whisk until lump-free. Spoon into the tin, then bake for 25–30 minutes until golden and risen and a skewer poked in to the centre comes out clean. Drizzle with some of the remaining coffee.

2 Cool in the tin while you stir the icing sugar into the mascarpone or soft cheese. Chill until the cake is cool, then spread over the icing, dust with a little cocoa and scatter with the chocolate-covered coffee beans. Cut into 15 squares to serve.

PER SQUARE 436 kcals, protein 5g, carbs 45g, fat 28g, sat fat 16g, fibre 1g, sugar 31g, salt 0.56g

Summer fruitbowl tartlets

These make a lovely addition to afternoon tea. To get ahead, you can bake the pastry cases and prepare the custard and fruits, but assemble the tartlets at the last minute.

TAKES 40 MINUTES, PLUS COOLING
• MAKES 8

300g ready-made shortcrust pastry
150ml tub double cream
200ml/7fl oz ready-made good-quality
   shop-bought vanilla custard
400g/14oz mixed summer fruits, such
   as small strawberries, raspberries,
   blueberries and redcurrants
icing sugar, for dusting
a few chopped pistachio nuts (optional)

1 Heat oven to 190C/170C fan/gas 5. Divide the pastry into eight equal pieces. Roll out each one to line a 7–8cm deep fluted tartlet tin, then trim, leaving a little pastry sticking up above the tin. Line each with a paper muffin case and add a layer of baking beans. Put on a baking sheet and bake for 10 minutes, then remove the paper and beans, and bake for a further 5 minutes until the pastry is crisp and golden. Remove from the tins and leave to cool on a wire rack.

2 Beat the cream until thick, then very gently fold in the custard.

3 Halve or quarter any large strawberries and remove the stalks from any redcurrants, then mix the fruits together.

4 Fill the pastry cases with the custard mixture and pile a generous layer of fruits on top. Dust thickly with icing sugar and scatter over some chopped pistachios, if you like.

PER TARTLET 281 kcals, protein 5g, carbs 32g, fat 15g, sat fat 6g, fibre 2g, sugar 14g, salt 0.46g

Lemon & poppy seed cupcakes

For an orange version, swap the lemon zest for orange zest in the cakes, and the juice in the icing for that of half an orange.

TAKES 1 HOUR, PLUS COOLING
● **MAKES 12**

225g/8oz self-raising flour
175g/6oz golden caster sugar
zest 2 lemons
1 tbsp poppy seeds, toasted
3 large eggs, beaten with a fork
100g/4oz natural yogurt
175g/6oz butter, melted and cooled a
   little, plus 225g/8oz butter, softened
400g/14oz icing sugar, sifted
juice 1 lemon
few drops yellow food colouring,
   icing flowers or yellow sprinkles,
   to decorate

1 Heat oven to 180C/160C fan/gas 4 and line a 12-hole muffin tin with cupcake cases. Mix the flour, sugar, zest and poppy seeds in a mixing bowl. Tip in the eggs, yogurt and melted butter. Mix, then divide among the cases. Bake for 20–22 minutes until a skewer poked in comes out clean. Cool for 5 minutes in the tin, then lift on to wire racks.
2 Beat together the softened butter, icing sugar and lemon juice. Add drops of food colouring. Spoon into a piping bag with a large star nozzle.
3 Hold the piping bag almost upright with the nozzle about 1cm from the cake. Pipe one circle of icing around the edge, then pipe a second, smaller spiral next to it that continues until there are no gaps in the centre. Slightly 'dot' the nozzle into the icing as you stop squeezing, to finish neatly. Ice all the cakes in this way, then top with sugar decorations or scatter with sprinkles.

PER CUPCAKE 529 kcals, protein 4g, carbs 66g, fat 30g, sat fat 18g, fibre 1g, sugar 51g, salt 0.75g

Beetroot brownies

Adding beetroot means you need nowhere near as much butter as with regular brownies, so not only are these delicious, they're lower in fat too!

TAKES 55 MINUTES • CUTS INTO 15–20 SQUARES

100g/4oz unsalted butter, diced, plus extra for greasing
200g bar plain chocolate, chopped
400g/14oz cooked beetroot (not dipped in vinegar!), roughly chopped
1 tsp vanilla extract
250g/9oz golden caster sugar
3 large eggs
100g/4oz plain flour
25g/1oz cocoa powder

1 Heat oven to 180C/160C fan/gas 4. Grease and line a 20 × 30cm traybake or roasting tin. Melt the chocolate in a bowl set over a pan of barely simmering water. Scrape into a food processor or blender with the butter, beetroot and vanilla. Whizz until the mix is as smooth as you can get it. The butter should melt as you do this.

2 Put the sugar and eggs into a large bowl, then beat with an electric hand whisk until thick, pale and foamy, about 2 minutes. Spoon the beetroot mix into the bowl, then use a large metal spoon to very gently fold it into the whisked sugar and eggs. Sift in the flour and cocoa powder, then gently fold these in to make a smooth batter.

3 Pour into the tin and bake for 25 minutes or until risen all over, with just the merest quiver under the centre of the crust when you shake the tin. Cool completely in the tin, then cut into squares.

PER BROWNIE (15) 255 kcals, protein 4g, carbs 32g, fat 13g, sat fat 7g, fibre 2g, sugar 24g, salt 0.11g

Cream tea tarts

No one will be able to resist these yummy little jam tarts. Using strawberry jam makes a nice play on a scone cream tea, but any berry jam will work well.

TAKES 45 MINUTES, PLUS COOLING
● **MAKES 18**

375g pack ready-made shortcrust
    pastry
flour for dusting
jar of strawberry jam
200ml tub clotted cream

1 Heat oven to 190C/170C fan/gas 5. Roll out the shortcrust pastry on a lightly flour-dusted surface to about £1 coin thickness. Stamp out eighteen 8cm rounds with a fluted cutter and use to line bun tins.

2 Fill each tart with 1 teaspoon of the jam – don't be tempted to fill them to the very top. Bake for 15–20 minutes until the pastry is cooked and the jam is bubbling. Cool completely in the tins.

3 Carefully remove the cooled tarts from the tins – the tip of a knife will help release them. Top each tart with a small dollop of clotted cream and serve.

PER TART 122 kcals, protein 1g, carbs 13g, fat 7g, sat fat 3g, fibre none, sugar 4g, salt 0.22g

Chocolate and Earl Grey torte

What better to serve at teatime but a chocolate cake infused with tea? This grown-up fudgy chocolate cake is also gluten- and wheat-free.

TAKES 1 HOUR, PLUS COOLING

● **CUTS INTO 10 SLICES**

200g/7oz butter, diced, plus extra for greasing
leaves from 2 Earl Grey tea bags
100ml/3½fl oz hot milk
250g/9oz good dark chocolate (we used a 78% cocoa solids bar)
140g/5oz ground almonds
6 large eggs, separated
200g/7oz caster sugar
cocoa powder and icing sugar, to dust
crème fraîche or cream, to serve

1 Heat oven to 180C/160C fan/gas 4. Grease and line the base and sides of a deep 22cm-round loose-bottomed tin so the paper comes about 2.5cm above the sides. Stir the tea leaves into the hot milk.
2 Melt the chocolate, butter and a pinch of salt together in a bowl set over a pan of barely simmering water. Then stir in the ground almonds, followed by the egg yolks and milky tea, including the leaves.
3 Beat the egg whites until stiff, then beat in the caster sugar until stiff-ish again. Stir a spoonful into the chocolate mixture to loosen the eggs, then gently fold in the rest with a big metal spoon or spatula. Scrape the mixture into the tin and bake for 30–35 minutes – the torte should still have a slight wobble. Cool completely in the tin.
4 Carefully remove from the tin and lift on to a serving plate. Dust all over with cocoa and icing sugar, then serve it with a dollop of crème fraîche or cream.

PER SLICE 514 kcals, protein 10g, carbs 34g, fat 37g, sat fat 17g, fibre 3g, sugar 29g, salt 0.39g

Zesty carrot & ginger loaf

If you like your ginger cake really dark, swap the golden syrup for more black treacle.

**TAKES 1 HOUR 25 MINUTES, PLUS
COOLING • CUTS INTO 8 SLICES**

100g/4oz unsalted butter, plus extra
    for greasing
100g/4oz dark muscovado sugar
50g/2oz black treacle
50g/2oz golden syrup
zest and juice 1 lemon and zest
    1 orange
1 large carrot, grated (you will need
    140g/5oz flesh)
5 balls stem ginger from a jar, finely
    chopped
175g/6oz self-raising flour
¼ tsp each bicarbonate of soda and
    ground black pepper
2 tsp ground ginger
2 large eggs
140g/5oz icing sugar, sifted

1 Heat oven to 180C/160C fan/gas 4. Butter and line a 900g loaf tin. Gently melt the butter, muscovado sugar, treacle, syrup and half the zests together into a large pan.

2 Add the carrot, three-quarters of the chopped ginger, the flour, bicarbonate of soda, pepper, ground ginger, eggs and ¼ teaspoon salt to the pan and stir to a smooth batter. Pour into the tin and bake for 45 minutes, or until dark brown and risen and a skewer inserted into the middle comes out clean. Cool for 20 minutes in the tin, then turn out on to a wire rack.

3 Mix the icing sugar and remaining zests with enough lemon juice (about 4 teaspoons should do it) to make a smooth, thick icing. When the cake is cool, spread the icing over the top and scatter with the reserved chopped ginger. Leave to set, then slice and serve.

PER SLICE 379 kcals, protein 4g, carbs 66g, fat 13g, sat fat 7g, fibre 1g, sugar 48g, salt 0.44g

Banana fairy cakes

Kids will love eating these as much as they love making them. If not eating them straight away, toss the sliced banana in lemon juice so it doesn't brown.

TAKES 35 MINUTES, PLUS COOLING
● **MAKES 8**

140g/5oz wholemeal flour
2 tsp baking powder
50g/2oz golden caster sugar
1 medium egg
50g/2oz melted butter, cooled
100ml/4fl oz semi-skimmed milk
2 small ripe bananas, 1 mashed,
    1 sliced
140g/5oz white chocolate, roughly
    chopped
ground cinnamon, for sprinkling

1 Heat oven to 190C/170C fan/gas 5. Line a bun tin with eight paper cases. In a large bowl, mix the flour, baking powder and sugar with a pinch of salt.
2 In another bowl beat the egg, melted butter and milk for 20 seconds; add the mashed banana and beat for 5 seconds more until everything is nicely mixed.
3 Pour the banana mix into the flour and fold everything together. When almost combined, add 85g/3oz of the chocolate – the mix will still look a little lumpy. Spoon into the paper cases and bake for 18–20 minutes until golden and risen. Cool on a wire rack.
4 Melt the remaining white chocolate over a pan of barely simmering water. Allow to cool a bit, then spread on top of the cakes. Add a couple of slices of banana and sprinkle with cinnamon.

PER CAKE 256 kcals, protein 5g, carbs 34g, fat 12g, sat fat 7g, fibre 2g, sugar 22g, salt 0.47g

Chocolate fudge cake

You can't beat a good chocolate cake, and this is really good. Brilliant for bake sales at school, and kids can decorate them however they want.

TAKES 1½ HOURS, PLUS COOLING

● **CUTS INTO 12 SLICES**

200g/7oz plain chocolate, broken into chunks (use one with a low cocoa content)

200g/7oz butter

200g/7oz light muscovado sugar

100ml/3½fl oz soured cream

2 large eggs, beaten

200g/7oz self-raising flour

5 tbsp cocoa powder

hundreds and thousands, to decorate

FOR THE ICING

100g/4oz plain chocolate

170g can condensed milk

100g/4oz butter

1 Heat oven to 160C/140C fan/gas 3. Line a 22cm-square baking tin. Put the chocolate, butter and sugar into a large pan with 100ml/3½fl oz hot water and gently melt. Set aside for 2 minutes, then stir in the soured cream and eggs. Stir in the flour and cocoa until lump-free, then pour the mixture into the tin. Bake for 50–55 minutes until a skewer comes out clean. Sit the tin on a wire rack to cool.

2 Gently melt together the icing ingredients in a heatproof bowl over a pan of barely simmering water. Chill or cool until spreadable.

3 To decorate, spread the icing over the cake and scatter with sprinkles. Cut the cake into triangles or fingers to serve.

PER SLICE 502 kcals, protein 6g, carbs 49g, fat 33g, sat fat 20g, fibre 1g, sugar 35g, salt 0.66g

Christmas tree crispy pops

Cover the kitchen table with a wipe-clean tablecloth or sheets of baking parchment and let the kids go mad with these!

TAKES 40 MINUTES, PLUS CHILLING

● **MAKES 6**

100g/4oz marshmallows

3 tbsp golden syrup

100g/4oz rice cereal/pops (we used
   Rice Krispies)

6 ice-cream cones

500g/1lb 2oz icing sugar

½ tsp green food colouring

lots of sweets and sprinkles,
   to decorate

1 Melt the marshmallows and golden syrup in a pan then stir in the rice cereal. Working quickly, pack the mixture into six ice-cream cones and push a lolly stick into the middle of each one. Chill the cones for 1 hour until firm.

2 Mix the icing sugar with the green food colouring and enough water to make a thick icing. Dip the cones into the icing and decorate with the sweets and sprinkles. Prop on a wire rack to set.

PER POP 547 kcals, protein 3g, carbs 132g, fat 0.4g, sat fat 0.1g, fibre 0.2g, sugar 112g, salt 0.40g

Cherry, choc & coconut traybake

This is so easy and only uses five ingredients. Little kids will love stirring the mixture together and pressing into the tin; big kids should be able to do the whole recipe.

TAKES 30 MINUTES ● CUTS INTO 16 SLICES

200g/7oz desiccated coconut
85g/3oz caster sugar
2 large eggs, beaten
200g bar white chocolate, roughly chopped
85g/3oz glacé cherries, halved

1 Heat oven to 180C/160C fan/gas 4. Line a 20 × 30cm baking tin with baking parchment. In a large bowl, mix the desiccated coconut, sugar, eggs, white chocolate and glacé cherries until combined. Transfer the mixture to the tin, gently smoothing the surface.
2 Cook for 20 minutes, until golden brown and set, then cool in the tin before slicing into 16 bars.

PER SLICE 187 kcals, protein 3g, carbs 17g, fat 13g, sat fat 9g, fibre 2g, sugar 17g, salt 0.07g

Sprinkle sandwich cake

Sticking the sprinkles around the middle is messy, so put the cake plate on a tray to catch any that escape.

TAKES 50 MINUTES, PLUS COOLING
- **CUTS INTO 8 SLICES**

140g/5oz butter, softened, plus extra
   for greasing
140g/5oz caster sugar
2 large eggs
140g/5oz plain flour
1 tsp baking powder
1–2 tsp milk

FOR THE FILLING

100g/4oz butter, softened
140g/5oz icing sugar, plus extra for
   dusting (optional)
2–3 tbsp strawberry or raspberry jam
hundreds and thousands, to decorate

1 Heat oven to 180C/160C fan/gas 4. Grease and line two 20cm-round sandwich tins. Beat the butter and sugar together with an electric whisk until fluffy. Beat in the eggs, followed by the flour and baking powder. Add enough milk to the mixture so that it falls off a spoon easily. Divide between the tins and bake for 20 minutes or until a skewer comes out clean. Turn the cakes out on to a wire rack and cool.
2 To make the filling, beat the butter until smooth, then gradually beat in the icing sugar. Spread the buttercream on one cake up to the edges. Spread a layer of strawberry or raspberry jam on top. Put the second cake on top and squash it down so the buttercream sticks out a bit. Press hundreds and thousands on to the buttercream with a teaspoon. Dust the top with icing sugar, if you like.

PER SLICE 439 kcals, protein 2g, carbs 55g, fat 25g, sat fat 16g, fibre none, sugar 41g, salt 0.58g

Peanut butter brownies

These are yummy and very, very easy to make. Eat cold for a snack with a glass of milk, or warm with ice cream for pudding.

TAKES 55 MINUTES • CUTS INTO 16 SQUARES

225g/8oz crunchy peanut butter
200g bar dark chocolate, broken into pieces
300g/10oz light soft brown sugar
3 medium eggs
100g/4oz self-raising flour

1 Set aside 50g/2oz each of the peanut butter and chocolate. Heat oven to 180C/160C fan/gas 4 and line a 20cm-square baking tin. Gently melt the remaining peanut butter, chocolate and all the sugar in a pan, stirring occasionally, until the sugar has just about melted. Turn off the heat and use a wooden spoon to beat in the eggs one by one. Stir in the flour and scrape into the tin.

2 Melt the reserved peanut butter either in the microwave on High for 45 seconds, or in a pan, until runny, then dot over the mix. Bake for around 30–35 minutes until it has a crust, but the middle still seems slightly uncooked.

3 Melt the reserved chocolate, drizzle over the brownie, then cool in the tin before cutting into 16 squares.

PER SQUARE 250 kcals, protein 6g, carbs 32g, fat 12g, sat fat 4g, fibre 1g, sugar 26g, salt 0.24g

Little lemon cupcakes

These little cupcakes are really easy to make, and just as easy to change too. Swap lemon for orange or add 2 tablespoons cocoa powder to make chocolate.

TAKES 40 MINUTES, PLUS COOLING
- **MAKES 12**

140g/5oz unsalted butter, softened
100g/4oz caster sugar
zest ½ lemon
2 large eggs, lightly beaten
140g/5oz self-raising flour

FOR THE BUTTERCREAM ICING

85g/3oz butter, softened
175g/6oz icing sugar
zest and juice ½ lemon
sprinkles or sweets, to decorate

1 Heat oven to 180C/160C fan/gas 4. Line a 12-hole bun tin with paper cases. Beat the butter and sugar in a big bowl with a wooden spoon until really soft, then add the lemon zest. Stir in the eggs, then the flour until it is all mixed. Use teaspoons to spoon the mixture among the cake cases. Bake for 18–20 minutes until the cakes are golden and springy when you touch them. Cool the cakes on a wire rack.

2 While you wait for the cakes to cool, make the buttercream icing. Beat the butter until it is really soft. Gradually beat in the icing sugar, lemon zest and juice until it is thick and yummy. Spread the buttercream on top of the cakes with the back of a spoon, then decorate with the sprinkles or sweeties.

PER CUPCAKE 289 kcals, protein 2g, carbs 34g, fat 17g, sat fat 10g, fibre none, sugar 25g, salt 0.24

Chocolate spider cookies

Make these for Halloween and give everyone a spooky treat!

TAKES 40 MINUTES, PLUS SETTING
● **MAKES 14**

200g/7oz dark or milk chocolate,
  broken into chunks
113g pack liquorice Catherine wheels
2 × 154g packs Oreo cookies
white and black icing pens

1 Melt the chocolate in a heatproof bowl set over a pan of barely simmering water. Once melted, turn off the heat and leave the chocolate in the bowl to keep warm while you make the spiders.

2 Unroll some of the liquorice wheels and cut into 2–3cm lengths to use as the spiders' legs.

3 Splodge a small teaspoon of the melted chocolate on to half the cookies. Arrange eight liquorice legs on top, then sandwich with another cookie. Spread some more chocolate on top of the second cookie to cover, then put them somewhere cool to set.

4 Use the icing pens to add eyes, by first blobbing two big dots of white icing on each, topped with two smaller dots of black icing.

PER COOKIE 201 kcals, protein 2g, carbs 30g, fat 9g, sat fat 5g, fibre 1g, sugar 23g, salt 0.32g

Carrot, courgette & orange cake

These garden cakes freeze really well so it's worth making two. Once cool, wrap them in foil then cling film and freeze for up to 3 months. Decorate after defrosting.

TAKES 1 HOUR, PLUS COOLING
- **MAKES 2 × 20CM CAKES, EACH CUTS INTO 8–10 SLICES**

250g pack butter, softened, plus extra for greasing
200g/7oz caster sugar
3 large eggs
250g/9oz self-raising flour
1 tsp bicarbonate of soda
zest 2 oranges
1 tsp ground mixed spice
100g/4oz carrot, grated
100g/4oz courgette, grated

FOR THE ICING
zest 1 orange, plus 2–3 tbsp juice
140g/5oz icing sugar

1 Heat oven to 180C/160C fan/gas 4. Grease and line the bases of two 20cm-round cake tins. Beat the butter, sugar, eggs, flour, bicarbonate of soda, zest and the mixed spice together, then stir in the carrot and courgette. Divide the mixture between the tins and bake for 20–25 minutes or until a skewer inserted comes out clean. Cool.
2 To make the icing, mix enough orange juice into the icing sugar to give a thick, but drizzly icing. Drizzle over the cakes, then scatter with the zest and leave to set completely.

PER SLICE (8) 273 kcals, protein 3g, carbs 35g, fat 14g, sat fat 9g, fibre 1g, sugar 23g, salt 0.54g

Rudolph's carrot flapjacks

Make these on Christmas Eve with the kids then leave them out for Rudolph with a bowl of milk and a glass of something a little stronger for Santa!

TAKES 1 HOUR 10 MINUTES
- **MAKES 16**

200g/7oz butter
100g/4oz golden syrup
50g/2oz light soft brown sugar
300g/10oz rolled oats
2 carrots, grated
zest 1 orange
100g/4oz dried apricots, chopped
1 tsp ground cinnamon
50g/2oz pumpkin seeds

1 Heat oven to 160C/140C fan/gas 3. Line an 18cm-square baking tin with baking parchment.
2 Melt the butter, golden syrup and sugar in a large pan. Mix in the rolled oats, grated carrots, orange zest, chopped apricots, cinnamon and pumpkin seeds. Stir everything together then pack into the prepared tin, pushing down well.
3 Bake for 40–45 minutes then cool in the tin before slicing into 16 squares.

PER SERVING 302 kcals, protein 6g, carbs 28g, fat 17g, sat fat 9g, fibre 3g, sugar 14g, salt 0.30g

Chocolate fudge

The boiling fudge gets very hot, so close supervision by an adult is a must. Once cooled, wrap the squares in cellophane for the authentic sweetshop look.

TAKES 30 MINUTES, PLUS SETTING
● **CUTS INTO 30–36 SQUARES**
397g can condensed milk
150ml/¼ pint milk
450g/1lb demerara sugar
100g/4oz butter
1 tbsp glucose syrup
100g/4oz plain chocolate

TO DECORATE
50g/2oz white chocolate, melted

1 Line an 18cm-square baking tin with baking parchment. Gently heat all the ingredients, except the plain and white chocolates, in a large non-stick pan, stirring until all the sugar dissolves.
2 Bring to the boil and simmer gently for about 15 minutes, stirring frequently with a wooden spoon. As the mixture thickens, stir and scrape the pan or it can catch on the bottom and you will get burnt bits in the fudge. Remove the pan from the heat and cool for 5 minutes.
3 Stir in the plain chocolate, then beat the fudge until thick and grainy, about 5 minutes. This is easiest with a pair of electric beaters. Spread into the prepared tin to cool. Once completely cold, cut the fudge into squares, then drizzle with the melted white chocolate to decorate. Store in an airtight container for up to 1 week.

PER SQUARE (30) 130 kcals, protein 1g, carbs 22g, fat 5g, sat fat 3g, fibre none, sugar 22g, salt 0.09g

Microwave banana pudding

Save over-ripe bananas for this recipe. Freeze them whole in plastic bags – the browner and softer the bananas, the stronger the flavour when baked.

TAKES 20 MINUTES • SERVES 4–6

100g/4oz butter, plus extra for greasing
2 ripe bananas
100g/4oz light muscovado sugar
100g/4oz self-raising flour
2 tsp ground cinnamon
2 large eggs
2 tbsp milk
icing sugar, to dust
toffee sauce and ice cream, to serve

1 Put the butter in a 1-litre baking dish and microwave on High for 30 seconds–1 minute until melted. Add 1½ of the bananas, mash into the melted butter, then add the sugar, flour, cinnamon, eggs and milk. Mix well.

2 Slice the remaining banana over the top, then return to the microwave and cook on High for 8 minutes until cooked through and risen. Serve warm, dusted with icing sugar, if you like, with toffee sauce and a scoop of ice cream.

PER SERVING 474 kcals, protein 7g, carbs 57g, fat 26g, sat fat 15g, fibre 1g, sugar 37g, salt 0.77g

Chocolate cupcakes

Look for lots of colourful sweets and sprinkles so the kids can get really creative with these fun cakes – perfect for birthday parties.

TAKES 1 HOUR, PLUS COOLING

● **MAKES 12**

200g/7oz butter
200g/7oz plain chocolate (under 70% cocoa solids is fine)
200g/7oz light soft brown sugar
2 large eggs, beaten
1 tsp vanilla extract
250g/9oz self-raising flour
Smarties, sweets and sprinkles, to decorate

FOR THE ICING

200g/7oz plain chocolate
100ml/3½fl oz double cream, not fridge-cold
50g/2oz icing sugar, sifted

1 Heat oven to 160C/140C fan/gas 3 and line a 12-hole muffin tin with cases. Gently melt the butter, chocolate, sugar and 100ml/3½fl oz hot water together in a large pan, stirring occasionally, then set aside to cool a little.

2 Stir the eggs and vanilla into the chocolate mixture. Then whisk in the flour until lump-free. Spoon into cases until just three-quarters full – you may have a little mixture left over but don't overfill. Set aside for 10 minutes, then put on a low shelf in the oven and bake for 20–22 minutes. Leave to cool.

3 For the icing, melt the chocolate in a heatproof bowl set over a pan of barely simmering water. Once melted, turn off the heat, stir in the double cream and icing sugar. Chill until spreadable, then decorate each cake.

PER CUPCAKE 505 kcals, protein 5g, carbs 59g, fat 29g, sat fat 17g, fibre 2g, sugar 44g, salt 0.51g

Name cookies

These make perfect place settings at a family gathering or kids' party, why not wrap them in cellophane and tie them with pretty ribbons once set?

TAKES 1 HOUR ● MAKES 10

FOR THE COOKIES
100g/4oz butter, softened
50g/2oz light muscovado sugar
25g/1oz golden caster sugar
1 medium egg
120g/4½oz self-raising flour
25g/1oz cocoa
100g/4oz mint-flavoured chocolate, roughly chopped

TO ICE AND DECORATE
1kg bag icing sugar, sifted
1 tsp peppermint extract
lots of sweets and different-coloured icing pens or tubes

1 Heat oven to 190C/170C fan/gas 5. Beat the butter, sugars and egg, then stir in the flour and chocolate chunks. Spoon 10 well-spaced rough blobs on to non-stick baking sheets. Bake for 12–14 minutes until just golden, but still quite pale and soft in the middle. Cool on the sheet for 5 minutes, then lift on to wire racks with a fish slice and leave to cool completely.

2 Mix the icing sugar with the peppermint extract and enough water to make a thick icing. Spread the icing over the cookies and create a border around the edges using sweets and coloured icing. Leave for 10 minutes for the icing to set before writing a name in the centre of each cookie using the icing pens. Leave to dry.

PER BISCUIT 604 kcals, protein 3g, carbs 119g, fat 12g, sat fat 7g, fibre 1g, sugar 111g, salt 0.30g

Wrap-your-own spring rolls

Ten large spring rolls might appear to be a few more than your family will eat, but once they get started, making two each just won't be enough.

TAKES 1 HOUR 10 MINUTES

● **MAKES 10**

300g pack cooked rice noodles

400g/14oz mixed vegetables, such as red peppers, beansprouts, carrots or Chinese leaf cabbage, thinly sliced or shredded

140g/5oz cooked peeled prawns

100g/4oz cooked chicken or duck, shredded

small piece ginger, finely chopped

splash light soy sauce

Chinese five-spice powder, for sprinkling

10 sheets filo pastry

1 egg, beaten

sesame seeds, for sprinkling (optional)

1 Heat oven to 200C/180C fan/gas 6. Give everyone their own mixing bowl and spoon. Let them choose which ingredients they want (noodles are essential) in their rolls. Add a bit of ginger, a splash of soy and sprinkling of five-spice to each bowl and mix everything together.

2 Lay a sheet of pastry in front of everyone. Spoon some filling down one side of each sheet of filo and brush beaten egg around the edges. Roll up by folding the ends over the filling, then rolling them up.

3 Put the rolls on to a baking sheet, seam side down, brush with more egg and sprinkle with sesame seeds, if you want. Bake for 20–25 minutes or until golden.

PER ROLL 202 kcals, protein 12g, carbs 32g, fat 4g, sat fat 1g, fibre 2g, sugar 8g, salt 2.04g

Mini vegetable frittatas

Great for supper, any leftovers are also lovely cold in lunchboxes the next day – as they are or sandwiched in a roll with salad and tomato sauce or chutney.

TAKES 45 MINUTES ● **MAKES 12**

8 large eggs
125ml pot single cream
4 spring onions, thinly sliced
3 courgettes, diced
1 red pepper, deseeded and diced
good pinch dried thyme
2 tbsp olive oil, plus extra for greasing
85g/3oz semi-dried tomatoes, diced
120g/4½oz Cheddar or Gruyère, diced
    into 1cm/½in cubes

1 Heat oven to 180C/160C fan/gas 4. Break the eggs into a bowl, then pour in the cream. Season then gently beat with a fork.

2 Fry the spring onions, courgettes, red pepper and thyme in the oil in a frying pan until the vegetables are light golden brown. Cool for 5 minutes, then stir in the tomatoes and cheese.

3 Grease a 12-hole muffin tin. Spoon some veg equally into the holes. (Save any extra veg to nibble on.) Using a small ladle or spoon, pour the egg mix over the veg (you may find it easier to transfer the egg mix to a large jug, then pour the mix on to the vegetables).

4 Bake for 25 minutes, until puffed, golden and set. Leave to cool for about 5 minutes, then gently run a round-bladed knife around the inside of each muffin hole. Carefully lift out or tip out and serve warm or at room temperature.

PER FRITTATA 178 kcals, protein 8g, carbs 2g, fat 15g, sat fat 5g, fibre 1g, sugar 2g, salt 0.50g

Full English pizza

If you like, quarter the dough before rolling it and let everyone make their own pizza with a full-English face!

TAKES 40 MINUTES ● SERVES 4–6
500g pack bread mix
flour, for dusting
a little sunflower oil, for greasing
6 tbsp passata
140g/5oz mushrooms, sliced
4 sausages, skinned and quartered
8 rashers streaky bacon, halved
4 medium eggs

1 Heat oven to 220C/200C fan/gas 7. Make up the bread mix according to the pack instructions. On a lightly floured surface, roll out to fit a lightly oiled 30 × 40cm baking sheet. Spread the passata over the base and dot over the mushrooms. Squeeze out chunks of sausagemeat from the skins into a roasting tin, and add the bacon. Cook for 20 minutes with the pizza at the top of the oven and the sausage and bacon tin below.

2 Remove the pizza from the oven and use a fork to scatter the sausage chunks and bacon over it. Crack the eggs over too. Return to the oven and cook for 5 minutes more, or longer depending how well cooked you like your eggs.

PER SERVING (4) 721 kcals, protein 33g, carbs 76g, fat 33g, sat fat 10g, fibre 7g, sugar 6g, salt 5.30g

Summer sausage rolls

When the weather is warm, bring some sunshine flavours into everyone's favourite afternoon tea and picnic snack.

TAKES 40 MINUTES • MAKES 20

2 large boneless skinless chicken
    breasts
1 garlic clove, crushed
3 rashers streaky bacon, thinly sliced
4 sun-dried tomatoes, chopped
handful basil leaves, chopped
375g pack ready-rolled puff pastry
flour, for dusting
1 egg yolk, beaten
25g/1oz sesame seeds

1 Whizz the chicken and garlic in a food processor until the chicken is minced. Tip in the bacon, sun-dried tomatoes and basil. Pulse for 5 seconds to just mix through. Season well.
2 Roll the pastry sheet out slightly on a lightly floured surface and cut in half lengthways. Spread half the chicken mixture along the middle of one of the pastry strips, then roll up the pastry, pinching the sides together to seal. Using a sharp knife, cut into 2.5cm-long pieces. Repeat with the remaining pastry strip.
3 Heat oven to 200C/180C fan/gas 6. Put the rolls on a large baking sheet. Brush with the egg, then sprinkle with the seeds. Bake for 20 minutes until golden and cooked right through.

PER ROLL 119 kcals, protein 6g, carbs 6g, fat 8g, sat fat 3g, fibre 1g, sugar none, salt 0.38g

Cheese & caramelised onion coburg

If the onion is getting too brown as the loaves cook, lay pieces of parchment over the top.

TAKES 50 MINUTES, PLUS RISING
● **MAKES 2 LOAVES, EACH CUTS INTO 6 WEDGES**

400g/14oz granary or wholemeal bread flour
100g/4oz strong white bread flour, plus extra for dusting
7g sachet easy-bake dried yeast
1 tbsp soft butter
1 large onion, cut into thin wedges
1 tbsp olive oil
1 egg, beaten
50g/2oz grated mature Cheddar

1 Mix the flours, yeast and 1½ teaspoon salt in a large mixing bowl. Rub in the butter. Make a dip in the centre, pour in 300ml/½ pint hand-warm water, then mix with a round-bladed knife until the mixture comes together as a soft dough. Gather into a ball with your hands.

2 Knead for 8–10 minutes on a very lightly floured surface until smooth and elastic. Cover with an upturned bowl and leave until doubled in size.

3 Fry the onion in the oil until lightly caramelised. Cool.

4 Knock back the dough by lightly kneading 3–4 times. Halve and shape into two balls. Flatten each into an 18cm round and put on large, lined baking sheets. Make six cuts to mark each round into six wedges. Cover with tea towels and leave until doubled in size.

5 Heat oven to 220C/200C fan/gas 7. Brush with egg and scatter over the onion and cheese. Bake for 30 minutes.

PER WEDGE 183 kcals, protein 7g, carbs 31g, fat 5g, sat fat 2g, fibre 2g, sugar 3g, salt 0.74g

Shepherd's pie pasties

This is a great way to use up any roast lamb or beef. Shred the meat into small pieces and add to the pan along with the stock.

TAKES 1 HOUR ● MAKES 4, SERVES 4–6 (KIDS COULD SHARE ONE)

1 onion, chopped
1 tbsp olive oil
250g/9oz extra-lean minced lamb
200ml/7fl oz hot lamb or chicken stock
1 tbsp sun-dried tomato purée
1 tbsp Worcestershire sauce
100g/4oz frozen peas
500g pack puff pastry
400g/14oz cold mashed potatoes
1 egg, beaten

1 Cook the onion in the oil for 5 minutes, then brown the lamb for 2–3 minutes. Stir in the stock, purée and Worcestershire sauce, bring to the boil, then simmer for 15 minutes until the liquid has evaporated. Remove from the heat. Add the peas and season.

2 Heat oven to 220C/200C fan/gas 7. Quarter the pastry, then roll each piece into an 18cm square. Divide the mash among the squares and top with the mince mixture. Dampen the edges of the pastry, pull the four corners up so they meet in the centre, then press the edges firmly together to seal.

3 Transfer to a baking sheet, brush with egg and bake for 20 minutes until golden.

PER PASTY 793 kcals, protein 26g, carbs 59g, fat 52g, sat fat 21g, fibre 5g, sugar 5g, salt 2.12g

Toad-in-the-hole

Serve with lots of gravy and your favourite vegetables, or some good old baked beans.

TAKES 1 HOUR ● SERVES 4

12 chipolata sausages
1 tbsp sunflower oil

FOR THE BATTER

140g/5oz plain flour
2 large eggs
175ml/6fl oz semi-skimmed milk

1 Heat oven to 220C/200C fan/gas 7. Put the sausages in a 20 × 30cm roasting tin with the oil, then bake for 15 minutes until browned.

2 Meanwhile, make up the batter mix. Tip the flour into a bowl with ½ teaspoon salt, make a well in the middle and crack both eggs into it. Use an electric whisk to mix it together, then slowly add the milk, whisking all the time. Leave to stand until the sausages are nice and brown.

3 Carefully remove the sausages from the oven and watch out because the fat will be sizzling hot – if it isn't, put the tin on the hob for a few minutes until it is. Pour in the batter mix, transfer to the top shelf of the oven, then cook for 25–30 minutes, until risen and golden.

PER SERVING 472 kcals, protein 19g, carbs 37g, fat 29g, sat fat 9g, fibre 2g, sugar 5g, salt 2.34g

Mini turkey & cranberry pies

These dinky pies are so versatile – try them with chopped ham and mustard, too.

TAKES 45 MINUTES ● MAKES 8
500g pack shortcrust pastry
plain flour, for dusting
250g/9oz shredded leftover turkey
8 tbsp double cream or crème fraîche
8 tsp cranberry sauce
1 egg, beaten

1 Roll out the pastry on a floured surface so that it's just thinner than a £1 coin. Cut out eight 10cm circles using a pastry cutter or small saucer, then cut eight 9cm circles for the lids – you may need to re-roll the trimmings. Push the larger circles into eight holes of a muffin tin, then divide the turkey, cream or crème fraîche and cranberry sauce among them. Season well and brush the edges with a little egg.

2 Put a lid on top of each and pinch the sides together to seal. Chill for 15–20 minutes.

3 Heat oven to 200C/180C fan/gas 6. Brush the tops with more egg, then bake for 25 minutes until the pastry is crisp and golden. Serve warm, or leave to cool and enjoy cold.

PER PIE 430 kcals, protein 15g, carbs 33g, fat 28g, sat fat 12g, fibre 1g, sugar 3g, salt 0.74g

Dill scones

Delicious served simply warm with butter or cream cheese, but for a special afternoon tea or lunch, add smoked salmon and cucumber pickle or salad.

TAKES 45 MINUTES • MAKES 7–8

200g/7oz plain flour, plus extra for dusting
200g/7oz wholemeal plain flour
1 tsp bicarbonate of soda
½ × 20g pack dill, finely chopped
50g/2oz unsalted butter, very cold and cut into cubes
300ml/½ pint milk, warmed, plus extra for brushing
1 tsp poppy seeds, to scatter

1 Heat oven to 230C/210C fan/gas 8 and lightly flour a baking sheet. Mix the flours, bicarbonate of soda, chopped dill and 1 teaspoon salt in a large bowl, then rub in the butter until it disappears. Tip in the milk and stir to a sticky dough.
2 Scrape the dough on to a floured surface, dust the dough and your hands with more flour, then fold the dough over 2–3 times to smooth a little. Pat into a 4cm-deep round. Use a 7cm cutter dusted with flour to stamp out scones. Press the trimmings together and repeat.
3 Put the scones on the baking sheet, brush with milk, scatter with poppy seeds, then bake for 15–18 minutes or until golden and well risen. Cool on a wire rack. As with all scones, these are best eaten on the day.

PER SCONE (8) 226 kcals, protein 7g, carbs 35g, fat 7g, sat fat 4g, fibre 3g, sugar 3g, salt 0.40g

Classic white loaf

Instead of using a loaf tin, you could shape this into either a large freeform loaf or individual rolls, and experiment with different flavours or glazes.

TAKES 1 HOUR 10 MINUTES, PLUS RISING ● MAKES 1 LOAF

500g/1lb 2oz strong white flour, plus extra for dusting
7g sachet fast-action yeast
a little sunflower oil, for greasing

1 Make the dough by tipping the flour, yeast and 1 teaspoon salt into a large bowl and make a well in the middle. Pour in most of 350ml/12fl oz lukewarm water and mix the flour and water together until combined to a slightly wet dough – add a splash more water if necessary.

2 Tip the dough on to a floured surface and knead for 10 minutes until elastic. Put in an oiled bowl, cover with cling film and leave until doubled in size.

3 Knock back the dough by tipping it back on to a floured surface and pushing the air out. Mould into a rugby-ball shape and put in a 900g loaf tin. Cover with a tea towel and leave for 30 minutes.

4 Heat oven to 220C/200C fan/gas 7. Dust the loaf with a little more flour, bake for 15 minutes, then reduce the heat to 190C/fan 170C/gas 5 and continue to bake for 30 minutes until the loaf sounds hollow when tapped on the base. Leave the bread on a wire rack to cool.

PER SERVING 111 kcals, protein 4g, carbs 24g, fat 1g, sat fat none, fibre 1g, sugar 1g, salt 0.31g

Mushroom & goat's cheese calzone

This easy calzone makes a lovely vegetarian meal for two, but once you've mastered this recipe, why not experiment with different fillings?

TAKES 30 MINUTES, PLUS RISING

● **SERVES** 2

220g pack pizza base mix
2 tsp olive oil
250g/9oz mixed mushrooms, such as chestnut, Portobello, porcini or shiitake
1 fat garlic clove, crushed
pinch chilli flakes
1 tsp rosemary leaves, finely chopped
1 tbsp half-fat crème fraîche
100g/4oz goat's cheese
rocket leaves, to serve (optional)

1 Make up the pizza dough according to the pack instructions. Meanwhile, make the filling. Heat 1 teaspoon of the oil in a large frying pan and fry the mushrooms until golden. Add the garlic, chilli and rosemary, and cook for 1 minute more. Stir in the crème fraîche and 1 tablespoon water, and remove from the heat.

2 Heat oven to 220C/200C fan/gas 7. Roll out the dough to a 30cm-diameter circle. Spread the mushroom mix across half of the circle, leaving a 2cm border from the edge, and scatter on the goat's cheese. Fold over and press to seal.

3 Brush with the remaining oil, transfer to a baking sheet and cook for 15–20 minutes until risen and golden. Cut in halves and serve with rocket, if you like.

PER SERVING 484 kcals, protein 20g, carbs 66g, fat 17g, sat fat 7g, fibre 7g, sugar 4g, salt 3.21g

Cornbread muffins

Great with soups or chilli, these gorgeous muffins are really best eaten warm and fresh, spread with butter.

TAKES 1 HOUR 10 MINUTES
- **MAKES 12**

85g/3oz melted butter, plus extra knob for frying
1 large sweetcorn, kernels sliced off
1 small onion, finely chopped
½ red chilli, deseeded and finely chopped
140g/5oz plain flour
140g/5oz polenta or cornmeal
2 tsp baking powder
50g/2oz strong Cheddar or vegetarian alternative, grated
2 large eggs
284ml pot buttermilk
100ml/3½fl oz milk

1 Heat oven to 200C/180C fan/gas 6 and brush a 12-hole muffin tin with some of the melted butter. Put the corn kernels in a pan with the onion, chilli and knob of butter. Gently fry for 5–10 minutes until golden and soft.

2 Mix together the flour, polenta, baking powder and Cheddar with 1 teaspoon salt in a large mixing bowl. Whisk together the eggs, buttermilk and milk, then stir into the dry ingredients with the remaining melted butter and the corn mixture. Divide among the muffin holes (they will be quite full) and bake for 25–30 minutes or until golden brown and cooked through – poke in a skewer to check. Best eaten warm.

PER MUFFIN 189 kcals, protein 6g, carbs 22g, fat 9g, sat fat 5g, fibre 1g, sugar 3g, salt 0.44g

Crab & leek pasties

We tend to think of a pasty as a snack, but adding a beautiful crabmeat filling makes these special enough to serve to friends.

TAKES 55 MINUTES, PLUS CHILLING
- **MAKES 4**

500g pack puff pastry
flour, for dusting
25g/1oz butter
140g/5oz leeks, washed and thinly
    sliced
pinch of saffron strands
250g/9oz crabmeat (white or brown,
    or a mix of the two)
small bunch parsley, roughly chopped
50g/2oz fresh white breadcrumbs
zest and juice 1 lemon
1 egg, beaten

1 Heat oven to 200C/180C fan/gas 6. Roll out the pastry on a lightly floured surface, then cut round a plate to make four 18cm circles. Put in the fridge for 10 minutes.
2 In the meantime, melt the butter in a frying pan. Cook the leeks for 5 minutes until soft. Soak the saffron in 1 tablespoon boiling water for 2 minutes. Tip the saffron and soaking liquid into the leeks and cook for 1 minute more.
3 Put the crabmeat in a bowl with the parsley, breadcrumbs, zest and lemon juice. Stir in the leeks and some seasoning then divide the mix among the pastry circles, spooning the filling on one half of the pastry. Brush one edge with egg then fold the pastry over, pressing the edges together. Brush the pasties with more egg and bake for 30–35 minutes until golden. Serve warm or at room temperature.

PER PASTY 684 kcals, protein 23g, carbs 49g, fat 45g, sat fat 21g, fibre 3g, sugar 3g, salt 2.39g

Malted walnut seed loaf

The loaf will stay fresh in an airtight container for 3 days or can be frozen for 1 month.

TAKES 1 HOUR, PLUS RISING • MAKES 1 LOAF

500g/1lb 2oz strong wholemeal flour, plus extra for dusting
7g sachet fast-action yeast
100g/4oz mixed seeds (we used a mix of linseeds, hemp seeds, pumpkin seeds and sesame seeds)
50g/2oz walnut pieces
a little sunflower oil, for greasing

1 Mix the flour, yeast and 1 teaspoon salt in a large bowl and make a well in the middle. Pour in most of 350ml/12fl oz lukewarm water and use your fingers or a wooden spoon to mix the flour and water together until combined to a slightly wet, pillowy workable dough.

2 Tip the dough on to a lightly floured surface and knead in most of the seeds and all the walnuts for at least 10 minutes until elastic. Put the dough in a clean oiled bowl, cover with oiled cling film and rise until doubled in size.

3 Tip the dough on to a floured surface and push the air out. Shape into a large round. Roll in the remaining seeds, then lift on to a baking sheet, cover with a tea towel and leave to double in size.

4 Heat oven to 220C/200C fan/gas 7. Bake the bread for 15 minutes, then reduce the heat to 190C/170C fan/gas 5 and continue to bake for 30 minutes until the loaf sounds hollow when tapped on the base. Leave on a wire rack to cool.

PER SERVING 172 kcals, protein 7g, carbs 28g, fat 4g, sat fat 1g, fibre 5g, sugar 1g, salt 0.43g

Full English frittata

The frittata is an Italian classic – however, we think it works really well with everything that we Brits enjoy for breakfast!

TAKES 45 MINUTES ● SERVES 4

8 eggs
50ml/2fl oz soured cream
2 tsp olive oil, plus extra for greasing
4 rashers bacon, cut into strips
12 button mushrooms, sliced
4 leftover cooked chipolatas, cut into
    bite-size pieces
6 leftover roast potatoes, cut into
    bite-size chunks
fresh bread and brown or tomato
    sauce, to serve

1 Heat oven to 180C/160C fan/gas 4. First of all, beat the eggs with a whisk in a bowl, then whisk in the soured cream and some seasoning.
2 Heat a non-stick pan, add the oil, then fry the bacon and mushrooms until caramelised and cooked through. Towards the end, toss in the leftover sausages and roast potato chunks, and allow them to heat up in the pan alongside the bacon and mushrooms.
3 Tip the contents of the pan into a small, lightly greased roasting tin, then pour over the egg mixture. Bake until the egg has risen slightly and set.
4 Serve with fresh bread and brown sauce (or tomato sauce to add a splash of colour).

PER SERVING 442 kcals, protein 24g, carbs 22g, fat 29g, sat fat 9g, fibre 2g, sugar 1g, salt 1.79g

Ploughman's cheese & tomato pockets

If you're going on a picnic, make these gorgeous bakes and you'll need nothing more than a bit of pickle and a bottle of something fizzy to wash them down with.

TAKES 40 MINUTES, PLUS RISING
● **MAKES 6**

300ml/½ pint semi-skimmed milk
25g/1oz butter
500g/1lb 2oz strong granary flour, plus extra for dusting
7g sachet fast-action yeast
oil, or greasing
2 tbsp wholegrain mustard
200g/7oz strong cheese, such as extra-mature Cheddar, grated
225g/8oz cherry tomatoes, halved

1 Warm the milk and butter in a pan until the butter melts. Set aside until just warm to the touch. Meanwhile, mix the flour, yeast and 1 teaspoon salt together. Mix the wet ingredients into the dry, then set aside for 10 minutes.

2 Turn the rested dough on to a floured surface and briefly knead until springy. Put into an oiled bowl, cover with oiled cling film and leave until doubled in size.

3 On a floured surface, roll out the dough to 40 × 30cm. Spread over the mustard, then scatter with two-thirds of the cheese. Fold the top third of the dough down, then the bottom third up. Cover and leave for 30 minutes.

4 Heat oven to 200C/180C fan/gas 6. Trim the ends, then slice the dough into six slices. Lift on to a floured baking sheet, cut-sides down. Tuck the bottom edges under a little, then push the tomatoes and remaining cheese into the tops. Bake for 25 minutes.

PER POCKET 479 kcals, protein 24g, carbs 57g, fat 19g, sat fat 10g, fibre 5g, sugar 6g, salt 1.78g

Chicken, ham & potato pie

This is the perfect way to use up leftover roast potatoes, but if you don't have any they are readily available from the chiller cabinet in supermarkets.

TAKES 1 HOUR 40 MINUTES
- **SERVES 4**

2 tbsp olive oil
400g/14oz boneless skinless chicken breast, cut into small chunks
140g/5oz thick sliced ham, roughly chopped
roughly 450g/1lb leftover roast potatoes, large ones halved
2 leeks, trimmed and sliced
1 heaped tbsp plain flour, plus extra for dusting
200ml/7fl oz white wine
400ml/14fl oz chicken stock
3 heaped tbsp crème fraîche
375g pack ready-rolled shortcrust pastry
beaten egg, to glaze

1 Heat half the oil in a large frying pan and brown the chicken for 5 minutes. Tip into a big pie dish, scatter over the ham and roast potatoes evenly.

2 Heat the remaining oil and soften the leeks for about 5 minutes, then stir in the flour for 1 minute. Stir in the wine and stock, bring to the boil, stirring, then bubble to a thick sauce. Stir in the crème fraîche and some seasoning, and pour over the pie filling.

3 Heat oven to 200C/180C fan/gas 6. Roll the pastry to fit the dish and put on top of the pie. Use a fork to crimp the edges and press the pastry to the dish. Poke a small hole in the middle. Brush with the egg, then cook for around 30–40 minutes, until golden.

PER SERVING 956 kcals, protein 46g, carbs 82g, fat 50g, sat fat 19g, fibre 5g, sugar 6g, salt 2.31g

Courgette, potato & Cheddar bread

This is more than just bread, it's lunch baked in a loaf. Serve with a sharp salad and enjoy in the afternoon sunshine.

TAKES 1 HOUR 35 MINUTES, PLUS RISING • CUTS INTO 6–8 CHUNKS

500g/1lb 2oz new potatoes
500g/1lb 2oz strong flour
7g sachet dried yeast
1 courgette
85g/3oz strong Cheddar (or vegetarian alternative), grated
few thyme sprigs
2 tbsp olive oil, plus extra for greasing
175–200ml/6–7fl oz hand-warm water

1 Boil the potatoes until just tender, then drain and cool a little. Put the flour and yeast into a large bowl. When the potatoes are cool enough to handle, coarsely grate half straight into the flour, tossing occasionally to coat.

2 Grate in half the courgette, add half of the cheese and strip in half of the thyme leaves. Add 1 tablespoon olive oil mixed with the water. Bring the dough together and knead for a couple of minutes. Put into a lightly oiled bowl, cover and leave in a warm place until doubled in size.

3 Grease a 20 × 30cm tin. Push the dough into the tin firmly, pushing out the air. Finely slice the remaining potatoes and courgette. Scatter over the top with the remaining thyme and poke in so the slices just stick out a little. Cover with oiled cling film and leave for 45 minutes.

4 Heat oven to 200C/180C fan/gas 6. Cover with the remaining oil and cheese, then cook for 50 minutes–1 hour.

PER CHUNK (8) 330 kcals, protein 10g, carbs 60g, fat 8g, sat fat 3g, fibre 3g, sugar 2g, salt 0.22g

Sausage, bean & cheese pasties

If you would like to freeze the pasties, completely cool and freeze them in a single layer on a flat tray, covered well. Once frozen, transfer them to a freezer bag and seal.

TAKES 1 HOUR, PLUS RISING
● **MAKES 12**
500g pack bread mix
8 sausages
2 × 420g cans baked beans
a little oil, for greasing
140g/5oz strong Cheddar, grated
1 egg, beaten

1 Prepare the bread mix according to the pack instructions. While the dough rises, make the filling. Skin the sausages and roll the meat into small meatballs, about six–eight per sausage. Heat a large non-stick frying pan and brown the sausages. Once they're all brown, return to the pan and pour in the beans. Mix to combine, then allow to cool a little.
2 Heat oven to 200C/180C fan/gas 6. Grease two or three baking sheets. Divide the dough into 12 and roll out each one to a 17cm circle. Keep the remaining dough covered with oiled cling film.
3 Taking each circle in turn, fill with a scoop of the bean mix and a little of the grated cheese. Fold in half, pressing well to seal. Crimp the edges then transfer to an oiled baking sheet. Keep covered with oiled cling film while you make the rest. Brush with the beaten egg and cook for 15–20 minutes until golden.
4 Remove and allow to cool slightly.

PER PASTY 348 kcals, protein 16g, carbs 38g, fat 16g, sat fat 6g, fibre 5g, sugar 6g, salt 2.4g

Cheesy garlic bread

This is one of those really useful sides that goes with so many family dishes, such as chilli con carne, soups or salads, and is ideal for serving at summer barbecues.

TAKES 1 HOUR, PLUS RISING • CUTS INTO 12 SQUARES

500g strong white bread flour, plus
    extra for dusting
7g sachet fast-action yeast
2 tbsp olive oil
1 tbsp clear honey
2 garlic cloves, crushed
25g/1oz soft butter
100g/4oz mature Cheddar, grated
handful thyme leaves

1 Mix the flour, yeast and 1 teaspoon salt in a large bowl. Mix 300ml/½ pint hand-hot water with the oil and honey in a jug, then pour into the dry mix, stirring all the time to make a soft dough.

2 Turn the dough out on to a lightly floured surface, then knead for about 5 minutes until the dough no longer feels sticky, sprinkling with a little more flour as you need it. Stretch it to fit a Swiss roll tin or big baking sheet.

3 Mix the garlic with the butter, then dot over the dough. Sprinkle over the cheese and snip over the thyme. Cover the bread with lightly oiled cling film, then leave in a warm place to rise for about 40 minutes.

4 Heat oven to 200C/180C fan/gas 6. Remove the cling film, then bake the bread for 30 minutes until golden and risen. Leave to cool for 10 minutes, then cut into 12 pieces and serve.

PER SQUARE 215 kcals, protein 7g, carbs 33g, fat 7g, sat fat 3g, fibre 1g, sugar 2g, salt 0.61g

Coronation pies

The name says it all; these gorgeous little savoury pies are a twist on Coronation chicken – perfect for serving at a truly British afternoon tea.

TAKES 45 MINUTES • MAKES 12

1 onion, chopped
1 tbsp olive oil
2 tbsp medium curry powder
3 tbsp mango chutney
140g/5oz cooked skinless chicken
    breast, diced into chunks
140ml/5fl oz soured cream
knob of butter
500g pack shortcrust pastry
flour, for dusting
1 egg, beaten
2 tbsp flaked almonds

1 Fry the onion in the oil until soft, then stir in the curry powder and cook for 1 minute more. Scrape into a bowl and stir in the mango chutney, chicken, soured cream and some seasoning.
2 Heat oven to 200C/180C fan/gas 6. Cut 24 strips of baking parchment as wide as the base of a 12-hole muffin tin and grease one side with a little butter. Criss-cross two strips into each hole of the muffin tin so the edges stick out.
3 Thinly roll out three-quarters of the pastry on a lightly floured surface. Stamp out 12 circles big enough to line the holes generously.
4 Divide the chicken filling among the pies. Roll out the remaining pastry and cut out 12 lids. Top each pie with a pastry lid, press together the edges to seal and roll down the excess pastry to make a lipped edge. Brush with beaten egg and scatter with almonds. Poke a fork in each then bake for 25 minutes.

PER PIE 281 kcals, protein 8g, carbs 23g, fat 19g, sat fat 8g, fibre 2g, sugar 4g, salt 0.57g

Index

Also available from BBC Books and *Good Food*

bbcgoodfood.com

Great-value family food

Nutty chicken curry

Easy weeknight suppers

Easy sweet & sour chicken

Smart entertaining

Sea bass with sizzled ginger, chilli & spring onion

Hundreds of desserts

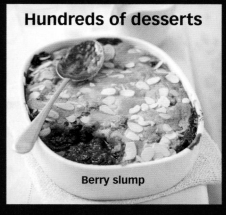

Berry slump

Over 6,000 recipes you can trust